FRY IT LIKE A PRO

THE ULTIMATE COOKBOOK FOR YOUR

T-FAL DEEP FRYER

An Independent Guide To The Absolute Best
103 Fryer Recipes You Have To Cook Before You Die

Eli Jacobs

Fry It Like A Pro The Ultimate Cookbook for Your T-fal Deep Fryer:
An Independent Guide to the Absolute Best 103 Fryer Recipes You Have To Cook Before You Die

Legal Disclaimer
The information contained in this book is the opinion of the author and is based on the author's personal experience and observations. The author does not assume liability whatsoever for the use of or inability to use any or all information contained in this book, and accepts no responsibility for any loss or damages of any kind that may be incurred by the reader as a result of actions arising from the use of information in this book. Use this information at your own risk. The author reserves the right to make any changes he or she deems necessary to future versions of the publication to ensure its accuracy.

Neither Eli Jacobs nor this book are affiliated with the manufacturers of T-fal products.

T-FAL ULTIMATE EZ CLEAN FRYER

Introduction

If you've purchased the T-Fal Ultimate EZ Clean Deep Fryer, you are probably aware of its reputation of being the easiest, most hassle-free deep fryer on the market. This appliance was designed to eliminate many of the problems commonly associated with fryers, such as the hassle factor and the mess. In addition, this appliance has many safety features, making it easy and safe to use in your kitchen. You are going to love creating fried dishes in your home using your T-Fal EZ Clean Fryer.

The T-Fal Fryer features an oil filtration system designed to alleviate the difficulty of draining and storing the oil between uses. With the flip of a switch, this simple system filters and drains the oil into a sealed storage container, where it can be placed in a dark space for later use. It features a filtering mechanism to help separate out the bits of breading and crumbs, leaving nothing but the oil for storing. This helps ensure that the oil does not smell or become rancid. The best part of this is that you no longer have to mess with trying to funnel the oil into a container yourself, often spilling and creating messy countertops. While you are enjoying your fried creations, the T-Fal will be doing its job of filtering and preparing your oil for storage.

Important Things to Know About Your Fryer

The T-Fal holds up to 3.5 liters of oil, meaning that it can fry up to 2.6 pounds of food safely. It is one of the best fryers on the market for maintaining its temperature throughout the frying process. This ensures that your food will achieve that delicious golden fried coating, with no mushy soft spots or burned bits. The adjustable thermostat makes it easy for you to select the exact temperature needed for whatever you may be frying. No more guessing games trying to heat oil on the stovetop!

The appliance is easy to use and assemble. It also has a breakaway power plug designed to fall away from the appliance in the event of someone tripping or becoming tangled in the cord. The cord simply disconnects from the appliance so the unit stays upright and no hot oil is spilled.

To clean up after using your fryer, simply drain the oil into the sealed storage container. All parts of the appliance, except for the heating element, are dishwasher safe. This makes for super easy clean-up, for what used to be a messy job. Simply wipe the heating element when it has cooled and your fryer will be ready to store or use again.

How to Use the T-Fal Ultimate EZ Clean

To prepare your fryer for use, select the "Fry" switch on the unit. Fill the removable bowl with oil somewhere between the minimum and maximum indicators.

Attach the power safety cord to the appliance and plug into the wall. Select the desired frying temperature using the adjustable thermostat. The temperature indicator light will turn on. Replace the lid while the oil heats. When the temperature indicator light switches off, the oil is ready to fry.

Lower the basket of food slowly into the oil. Place the lid back on the appliance and set timer for desired amount of time. Check periodically, turning items if necessary.

When frying is complete, lower the temperature on the thermostat. Lift the basket and hang on the clips to drain excess oil back into the bowl. When the oil has drained, remove the basket and serve the food hot.

To put away and store your fryer after use, unplug the appliance from the wall. Allow to sit for 2 hours for the oil to cool. When the oil has cooled, flip the switch to "Automatic Oil Filtration" position. The oil will be filtered into the sealed container for storage. To remove the container after filtration is complete, flip the switch to "Oil Box" and remove. Store the box horizontally in a dry, dark place until further use.

TABLE OF CONTENTS

Breakfast

BREAKFAST POCKETS

These easy little pockets are a great breakfast for on-the-go. They can be customized to your tastes by adding your favorites. Throw in a handful of spinach, tomato, or extra cheese. Any way you make them, these are sure to be a favorite for busy mornings.

Ingredients:

- 4-6 eggs
- Salt and freshly ground black pepper, to taste
- 2 tablespoons butter
- 1 pound cooked breakfast sausage
- ½ pound cooked bacon, crumbled
- 2 (8-ounce) containers Pillsbury Grands Flaky Layers Biscuits
- 1 cup cheddar cheese, shredded
- 1 cup frozen hash browns, defrosted

Preparation time: 15 minutes
Cooking time: 15 minutes

Directions:

1. Prepare fryer and set the temperature to 356 degrees. Cover the fryer with the lid.
2. In a bowl, add eggs, salt, and black pepper and beat well. Set aside.
3. In a deep frying pan, melt butter and heat sausage for about 2-3 minutes. Add bacon and stir to combine. Stir in hash browns.
4. Add egg mixture and cook for about 2-3 minutes or until desired doneness. Sprinkle cheese on top evenly and remove from heat.
5. Roll out each biscuit until they are all flat. With a small spoon, place sausage/ egg mixture on each biscuit, keeping filling to one side. Fold biscuits over filling and crimp the edges tightly to seal.
6. When the temperature indicator light has turned off, add the sausage and egg pockets and fry for about 4-5 minutes or until golden and puffy, flipping occasionally.
7. With a slotted spoon, transfer the pockets onto a paper towel-lined plate to drain.
8. Serve warm.

STUFFED FRENCH TOAST

This breakfast is a delicious, ideally served for special occasions or when you have plenty of time to enjoy, maybe while sipping a warm beverage. Be sure to use thick Texas style toast, as other pre-sliced breads will be too thin to slice. Squeeze in as much or as little cream cheese filling as you like, just be careful not to overfill and break the bread. Sprinkled with powdered sugar, this the perfect meal to serve to someone special.

Ingredients:

- 4 ounces cream cheese, softened
- 3 tablespoons powdered sugar, plus more for sprinkling
- ¼ teaspoon almond extract
- 10 thick bread slices, such as Texas toast
- 1 cup all-purpose flour
- 1½ teaspoons baking powder
- ½ teaspoon ground cinnamon
- 1/8 teaspoon ground nutmeg
- ½ teaspoon salt
- 2 eggs
- 1 cup milk

Preparation time: 20 minutes
Cooking time: 20 minutes

Directions:

1. Prepare fryer and set the temperature to 338 degrees. Cover the fryer with the lid.
2. In a bowl or stand mixer, add cream cheese, 3 tablespoons of powdered sugar, and almond extract and beat until fluffy.
3. Fit a large tip onto a pastry bag. Fill pastry bag with cream cheese mixture.
4. With a sharp bread knife, cut each bread slice into half diagonally.
5. With the tip of knife, gently make a 1-2 inch slice lengthwise into the center of each bread slice (make sure the slice runs parallel to the top and bottom of the bread).
6. Insert the pastry bag tip into the opening and squeeze out about 1 teaspoon of filling. With your thumb and finger, gently pinch the opening to seal.
7. In a bowl, mix together flour, baking powder, spices, and salt. Add eggs and milk and beat until smooth. Transfer batter mixture into a shallow, wide bowl. Dip each slice of prepared bread into the batter, coating both sides evenly.
8. When the temperature indicator light has turned off, add the bread into the oil carefully. Fry on each side until lightly browned.
9. With a slotted spoon or tongs, transfer the French toast onto a paper towel-lined plate to drain. Repeat with all remaining slices of bread.
10. Sprinkle with powdered sugar and serve immediately.

FRENCH TOAST STICKS

These little sticks are perfect for dipping in maple syrup. Loved by both kids and adults, they can be made with any thick bread such as French bread or brioche. Using bread that is a day or two old helps the sticks stay formed when they are fried.

Ingredients:

- 8 (¾-inch thick) slices day-old brioche
- 2 cups all-purpose flour
- 1½ cups sugar
- 1½ teaspoons baking powder
- ¾ teaspoon ground cinnamon
- ½ teaspoon ground ginger
- ¼ teaspoon nutmeg, freshly grated
- Pinch of ground cloves
- 2 large eggs
- 2 cups buttermilk
- 1 teaspoon vanilla extract
- Confectioners' sugar, for dusting
- Maple syrup, for serving
- Fresh fruit (of your choice), for serving

Preparation time: 15 minutes
Cooking time: 5 minutes

Directions:

1. Prepare fryer and set the temperature to 338 degrees. Cover the fryer with the lid.
2. Arrange a rack on a baking sheet. Set aside.
3. Cut each bread slice into thirds to make sticks.
4. In a large bowl, mix together flour, sugar, baking powder, and spices.
5. In another bowl, add eggs, buttermilk, and vanilla extract and beat until well combined. Add egg mixture into flour mixture and gently stir until combined.
6. Coat bread sticks in the batter evenly and place bread sticks onto wire rack over baking sheet to drain excess batter.
7. When the temperature indicator light has turned off, add the bread sticks into the oil carefully and fry for about 3 minutes. Flip and fry for about 1-2 minutes more or until golden brown.
8. With a slotted spoon, transfer the bread sticks onto a paper towel-lined plate to drain.
9. Dust with confectioners' sugar and drizzle with maple syrup. Serve immediately with your favorite fruit.

SAUSAGE

Just when you thought sausage couldn't get any tastier…we added it to the deep fryer. Rolled in cheesy breadcrumbs, this dish could really be served up at any time of day, but breakfast seemed like the ideal place to add this meal. After all, it may take the rest of the day to burn off those calories, but life is short!

Ingredients:

- 1 cup Parmesan cheese, finely grated
- 2 cups Italian breadcrumbs
- 3 eggs
- 1 pound Italian sausage roll, cut in 1½-2 inch pieces

Preparation time: 15 minutes
Cooking time: 5 minutes

Directions:

1. Prepare fryer and set the temperature to 356 degrees. Cover the fryer with the lid.
2. In a large bowl, mix together cheese and bread crumbs.
3. In another large bowl, add eggs and beat well.
4. Dip sausage pieces into eggs and then coat with cheese mixture evenly.
5. When the temperature indicator light has turned off, fry sausage pieces for about 4-5 minutes or until done completely.
6. With a slotted spoon, transfer the sausage pieces onto a paper towel-lined plate to drain.
7. Serve immediately.

SCOTCH EGGS

Scotch Eggs is a dish that comes from the United Kingdom. It consists of a soft boiled egg, wrapped in breaded sausage, and then fried. I think these make a perfect grab and go breakfast, with plenty of protein to help your day get off to a great start. Serve with a side of gravy or your favorite dipping sauce.

Ingredients:

- 10 extra large eggs, divided
- 1 pound breakfast pork sausage, raw, casing removed
- ¾ pound ground pork
- ¼ cup mixed fresh herbs (chives, sage, parsley, and thyme), chopped
- 1 tablespoon Dijon mustard
- ¼ teaspoon nutmeg, freshly ground
- Kosher salt and freshly ground black pepper, to taste
- 6 tablespoons all-purpose flour
- 1 tablespoon milk
- 2 cups panko breadcrumbs

Preparation time: 20 minutes
Cooking time: 15 minutes

Directions:

1. Prepare fryer and set the temperature to 356 degrees. Cover the fryer with the lid.
2. In a large pan, add 8 eggs and enough water to cover. Place over medium-high heat and bring to a boil. Reduce heat to low and simmer for about 4 minutes.
3. Drain the eggs and transfer into a large bowl of ice water for at least 10 minutes. Drain the eggs again, and then peel them.
4. In a bowl, add sausage, ground pork, herbs, mustard, nutmeg, and a pinch of salt and pepper. With your hands, mix until well combined. Make 8 equal sized balls from mixture.
5. In a shallow bowl, mix together flour and a good pinch of salt and black pepper.
6. In a second shallow bowl, add remaining 2 eggs and milk and beat well. In a third shallow bowl, place breadcrumbs.
7. Place meatballs onto a square of plastic wrap on a smooth surface. Place another piece of plastic wrap on top and flatten meatballs until large enough to cover the boiled eggs. Remove the plastic wrap from top.
8. Coat each egg with flour evenly. Place 1 egg in the center each meat portion. With damp hands, carefully shape meat mixture around egg.
9. Coat each covered egg with flour. Now, dip each egg into egg mixture and then coat with breadcrumbs. Again, dip into egg mixture and then coat with breadcrumbs.
10. When the temperature indicator light has turned off, fry the eggs in batches for about 5-7 minutes or until golden brown on all sides.
11. With a slotted spoon, transfer the eggs onto a paper towel-lined plate to drain.
12. Serve immediately with a sprinkling of salt.

GLAZED DONUTS

Who can resist a gooey, glazed donut, especially when it is still warm from the fryer? The only thing more fun than making your own donuts at home is eating the donuts you make yourself. Be sure to save the little pieces of dough from the center of the donuts to make donut holes. Coat them in the extra glaze or dust with powdered sugar.

Ingredients:

For Donuts:

- ¼ cup warm water (105-115 degrees)
- 2 (¼-ounce) envelopes active dry yeast
- 5 cups all-purpose flour, divided
- 2 eggs
- 1½ cups lukewarm milk
- ½ cup white sugar
- 1/3 cup shortening
- 1 teaspoon salt

For Glaze:

- 1/3 cup butter
- 2 cups confectioners' sugar
- 1½ teaspoons vanilla extract
- 4 tablespoons hot water

Preparation time: 15 minutes
Cooking time: 5 minutes

Directions:

1. Prepare fryer and set the temperature to 356 degrees. Cover the fryer with the lid.
2. In a bowl, add warm water and sprinkle with yeast. Set aside for about 5 minutes or until foamy.
3. In a large bowl, add yeast mixture, 2 cups of flour, eggs, milk, sugar, shortening, and salt and with an electric mixer, mix on low speed for a few minutes. Add remaining 3 cups of flour, ½ cup at a time, and beat until a dough is formed.
4. Now, with your hands, knead the dough for about 5 minutes or until smooth and elastic. Place dough in a greased bowl and cover with plastic wrap. Place the bowl in a warm place until dough doubles in size.
5. Place dough onto a floured surface and gently roll into ½-inch thickness. With a floured donut cutter, cut donuts from rolled dough. Cover loosely with a cloth and keep aside until the donuts have doubled in size.
6. For glaze: In a pan, melt butter over medium heat. Add confectioners' sugar and vanilla extract and stir until smooth. Remove from heat and stir in hot water, 1 tablespoon at a time until a thin mixture is formed.
7. When the temperature indicator light has turned off, fry donuts for about 2-3 minutes or until golden brown on both sides.
8. With a slotted spoon, place donuts onto a wire rack to drain.
9. Coat hot donuts with glaze evenly and place back onto the wire rack to drain off any excess glaze.

APPLE FRITTERS

As a kid, my Mom's favorite breakfast splurge was an apple fritter. So when I got my fryer I decided to surprise her with the homemade variety. She said they were some of the best she's ever tasted. Trust me, she wasn't just being polite. Serve with the cinnamon-flavored syrup or a very light sprinkling of cinnamon and sugar.

Ingredients:

- ½ cup milk
- 1 large egg
- 1 cup sweet apple, peeled, cored, and chopped
- 1 cup all-purpose flour
- 1 teaspoon baking powder
- ½ cup plus 1 tablespoon sugar, divided
- 1¼ teaspoons ground cinnamon, divided
- ¼ teaspoon salt
- ½ cup maple syrup

Directions:

1. Prepare fryer and set the temperature to 356 degrees. Cover the fryer with the lid.
2. In a bowl, add milk and egg and beat until well combined. Add chopped apple and gently stir to combine.
3. In another bowl, mix together flour, baking powder, 1 tablespoon of sugar, ¼ teaspoon of cinnamon, and salt. Add flour mixture to egg mixture and mix until just moistened.
4. When the temperature indicator light has turned off, place a heaping spoonful of the apple mixture into the fryer and cook for about 4 minutes, flipping occasionally.
5. With a slotted spoon, transfer the fritters onto a paper towel-lined plate to drain.
6. Repeat with remaining mixture.
7. In a sealable plastic bag, place remaining ½ cup of sugar and ¾ teaspoon of cinnamon. Add fritters, 2 at a time. Seal the bag and shake to coat well.
8. Transfer fritters onto serving plates.
9. In a microwave-safe bowl, mix together maple syrup and remaining ½ teaspoon of cinnamon and microwave on High for about 30 seconds.
10. Drizzle syrup over fritters and serve.

Preparation time: 15 minutes
Cooking time: 20 minutes

SAUSAGE PANCAKE BREAKFAST BITES

My kids used to love "breakfast corndogs" or sausage wrapped in pancakes on a stick. We love this recipe for sausage bites that are easy for little fingers to handle. Don't worry, adults love them, too. Serve with a side of maple syrup for dipping.

Ingredients:

- 1 cup flour
- 3 teaspoons baking powder
- 1 tablespoon brown sugar
- 1 tablespoon cinnamon sugar
- ¼ teaspoon salt
- 1 egg
- ¾ cup milk
- 2 tablespoons vegetable oil
- ½ teaspoon vanilla extract
- 1 bag mini pre-cooked sausage meatballs, or breakfast sausages cut into 1-2 inch sections
- Maple syrup, for serving

Preparation time: 15 minutes
Cooking time: 15 minutes

Directions:

1. Prepare fryer and set the temperature to 356 degrees. Cover the fryer with the lid.
2. In a bowl, mix together flour, baking powder, sugars, and salt.
3. In another large bowl, add egg and beat until fluffy. Add flour mixture, milk, oil, and vanilla extract and beat until well combined.
4. On a microwave-safe plate, place meatballs and microwave for about 60-90 seconds. Insert 1 toothpick into each meatball and coat with egg mixture evenly.
5. When the temperature indicator light has turned off, fry meatballs for about 1-2 minutes or until golden brown.
6. With a slotted spoon, transfer the meatballs onto a paper towel-lined plate to drain.
7. Serve immediately with maple syrup.

CHICKEN FRIED BACON WITH GRAVY

This is a fun recipe to use any time. My favorite way to serve these is with a bit of gravy spooned into a shot glass with a piece of bacon dipped in the gravy.

Ingredients:

For Bacon:

- ½ cup milk
- 1 egg
- ½ cup flour
- Garlic powder, to taste
- Salt and freshly ground black pepper, to taste
- 1 pound thick-sliced bacon, cut in half

For Gravy:

- 3 tablespoons butter
- 3 tablespoons flour
- 2 cups milk
- 2 tablespoons heavy cream
- Salt and freshly ground black pepper, to taste

Preparation time: 15 minutes
Cooking time: 10 minutes

Directions:

1. Prepare fryer and set the temperature to 374 degrees. Cover the fryer with the lid.
2. In a bowl, add milk and egg and beat until well combined.
3. In another bowl, mix together ½ cup flour, garlic powder, salt, and black pepper.
4. Dip bacon slices in egg mixture and then coat with flour mixture. Repeat this coating process one more time.
5. When the temperature indicator light has turned off, fry bacon slices for about 4 minutes or until golden brown.
6. With a slotted spoon, transfer bacon slices onto a paper towel-lined plate to drain.
7. For gravy: In a pan, melt butter over medium-high heat. Add flour and beat until well combined. Reduce heat to medium and cook for about 2-3 minutes. Remove from heat and slowly add milk, beating continuously.
8. Return the pan to heat and cook until gravy becomes thick, beating continuously.
9. Remove from heat. Add cream, salt, and black pepper and beat until well combined.
10. Serve bacon slices with gravy.

GRIT PATTIES

Grits are synonymous with the South, and I suppose deep frying is as well. So it makes perfect sense that the two should be paired. I first had a variation of these fried grit patties at a restaurant in my hometown, and enjoyed them so much that I went home and tinkered with making my own. The end result is quite tasty and I know you'll enjoy them as much as I do. You can even insert Popsicle sticks into each patty, for a fun serving idea at a party.

Ingredients:

- 5 cups water
- 3 tablespoons butter
- Salt, to taste
- 1½ cups grits
- ½ cup andouille sausage, finely chopped
- 4 tablespoons cheddar cheese, shredded
- 1 tablespoon freshly ground black pepper
- ¾ cup milk
- 1 egg
- 1 cup flour
- 1 cup Italian seasoned breadcrumbs

Directions:

1. Prepare fryer and set the temperature to 356 degrees. Cover the fryer with the lid.
2. In a 1-quart pan, add water and bring to a rolling boil. Add butter and salt and stir to combine. Add grits and stir to combine. Reduce heat to low and simmer for about 30-45 minutes or until cooked through, stirring occasionally.
3. Remove from heat and immediately stir in sausage, cheese, and black pepper. Transfer hot grits mixture onto a sheet pan and, with the back of a spoon, smooth into ¾-inch thickness. Refrigerate to cool overnight.
4. With a 3-inch round cookie cutter, cut 8 patties from grit mixture.
5. In a shallow bowl, add milk and egg and beat until well combined. In a second shallow dish, place flour. In a third shallow bowl, place breadcrumbs.
6. Dip each patty into egg mixture evenly. Coat with flour and then dip back into egg mixture. Now, coat with breadcrumbs evenly.
7. When the temperature indicator light has turned off, fry patties for about 4-5 minutes, flipping once halfway.
8. With a slotted spoon, transfer the patties onto a paper towel-lined plate to drain.
9. Serve immediately.

Preparation time: *15 minutes*
Cooking time: *55 minutes*

EXTRA CRUNCHY WAFFLES WITH STRAWBERRIES & CREAM

If you are looking for a simple way to dress up your everyday breakfast routine, then look no further. This recipe uses pre-packaged waffles, although you could certainly use your favorite homemade variety. Adding them to the fryer makes them extra crunchy and flavorful. Scoop on the easy fruit topping and you'll have a delicious breakfast in no time at all.

Ingredients:

- ½ cup fresh strawberries
- 1 teaspoon sugar
- 2 Eggo waffles (or your choice)
- Powdered sugar, for sprinkling
- Whipped cream, for topping
- Chopped walnuts, for topping

Preparation time: 15 minutes
Cooking time: 8 minutes

Directions:

1. Prepare fryer and set the temperature to 338 degrees. Cover the fryer with the lid.
2. In a bowl, add strawberries and sprinkle with 1 tsp sugar. Refrigerate until serving.
3. When the temperature indicator light has turned off, add the Eggo waffles and cook for about 6-8 minutes.
4. Transfer waffles onto a serving plate and immediately sprinkle with powdered sugar.
5. Place strawberries and juice on the fried waffle.
6. Top with a dollop of whipped cream. Sprinkle with walnuts and serve.

Appetizers

INDIAN SAMOSA

These delicious pockets offer a way to carry some hearty goodness with you in a portable snack. Filled with flavorful, spiced vegetables, these little pastries are a perfect lunch on the go.

Ingredients:

For Dough:

- 1 pound all-purpose flour (about 3-1/3 cups)
- ½ teaspoon baking soda
- 1 teaspoon cardamom seeds
- 1 teaspoon salt
- 4 tablespoons ghee (clarified butter)
- 2 tablespoons plain yogurt
- ¾ cup water

For Filling:

- 3 tablespoons sunflower oil
- 1 large onion, finely chopped
- 1 (1-inch) piece fresh ginger, finely grated
- 2 garlic cloves, finely minced
- ½ pound fresh peas, shelled
- 1 large carrot, peeled and finely chopped
- 1 green hot pepper, seeded and cut into thin strips
- 5 medium potatoes, boiled and mashed
- ½ bunch fresh cilantro, finely chopped
- 1 teaspoon garam masala
- 1 teaspoon ground cumin
- ½ teaspoon ground cardamom seeds
- ½ teaspoon ground coriander
- ½ teaspoon ground turmeric
- Salt and freshly ground black pepper, to taste

For Glue:

- 3-4 tablespoons hot water
- 3 tablespoons flour

Preparation time: 25 minutes
Cooking time: 25 minutes

Directions:

1. Prepare fryer and set the temperature to 356 degrees. Cover the fryer with the lid.
2. For dough: In bowl of a stand mixer, mix together flour, baking soda, cardamom seeds, and salt.
3. Add ghee and yogurt and mix until a sandy textured dough is formed. Add ½ cup of water and, with the dough hook, mix for about 4 minutes. Slowly, add remaining ¼ cup of water and mix until dough becomes soft, smooth, and elastic.
4. Make a ball from dough and coat with a little oil evenly. With a cloth, cover the dough ball and set aside at room temperature for about 1 hour.
5. For filling: In a skillet, heat oil over medium heat and sauté onion for about 2 minutes. Add ginger and garlic and sauté for about 1 minute.
6. Add peas, carrot, and hot pepper and stir to combine. Reduce heat to low and cook for about 5 minutes. Stir in mashed potatoes, cilantro, and spices and cook, covered, for about 5 minutes.
7. Remove from heat and set aside to cool.
8. For glue: In a bowl, add water and flour and beat vigorously until a thick cream-like mixture is formed.
9. Divide dough into 8 equal pieces. Roll 1 piece between the palms of your hand to form a smooth ball. Place dough ball onto a lightly floured smooth surface and roll until thin. Carefully, cut rolled dough in half to get 2 half circles.
10. With your fingers, spread some glue along the edges of the half circle. Fold in half, keeping the flat side open to form a cone and stuff with filling mixture. With your fingers, press the edges of each cone to seal.
11. Repeat with remaining dough pieces and filling mixture.
12. When the temperature indicator light has turned off, fry samosas for about 8-10 minutes or until golden brown on all sides.
13. With a slotted spoon, transfer the samosas onto a paper towel-lined plate to drain.
14. Serve immediately.

CRAB RANGOON

Crab Rangoon is one of my favorite appetizers to order at a Chinese restaurant. The crispy outside layer gives way to a creamy, warm inside with just a hint of crab. They are very easy to make right in your own kitchen. Serve with a side of duck sauce or sweet and sour.

Ingredients:

- 8 ounces light cream cheese, softened
- 3 ounces fancy crab meat, drained and crumbled
- 2 scallions, finely chopped
- 1 teaspoon garlic, minced
- 2 teaspoons Worcestershire sauce
- ½ teaspoon soy sauce
- 1 (12-ounce) package wonton wrappers

Preparation time: **20** *minutes*
Cooking time: **2** *minutes*

Directions:

1. Prepare fryer and set the temperature to 374 degrees. Cover the fryer with the lid.
2. In a bowl, add all ingredients except wrappers and mix until well combined.
3. Spread wrappers out on a smooth surface.
4. Place 1 heaping teaspoon of crab mixture in center of each wonton wrapper. With wet fingers, slightly moisten the edges of wonton. Fold the wrapper in a triangle shape and press to seal.
5. Pull the right and left corners up, attaching them to seal on top.
6. Repeat with remaining wrappers and filling mixture.
7. When the temperature indicator light has turned off, fry dumplings for about 1-2 minutes or until golden brown on all sides.
8. With a slotted spoon, transfer the dumplings onto a paper towel-lined plate to drain.
9. Serve immediately.

MUSHROOMS

I've found that sometimes even people who claim to dislike mushrooms will gobble up a helping of these babies. Be sure to pat your mushrooms dry before coating in flour to prevent the insides from getting too doughy. Some ideas for dipping sauces are ranch dressing, marinara sauce, or a creamy horseradish sauce. Any way you serve them, they are sure to be a hit.

Ingredients:

- 2 (8-ounce) packages mushrooms
- 1 cup flour, divided
- ½ cup Italian style breadcrumbs
- 1 tablespoon seasoned salt
- ½ tablespoon garlic salt
- ½ tablespoon ground black pepper
- 2-3 eggs

Preparation time: 15 minutes
Cooking time: 5 minutes

Directions:

1. Prepare fryer and set the temperature to 374 degrees. Cover the fryer with the lid.
2. Wash mushrooms and pat completely dry with paper towels.
3. In a gallon-sized bag, place mushrooms and ½ cup of flour. Seal the bag and shake until the mushrooms are coated with flour evenly.
4. In a shallow bowl, crack eggs and beat lightly.
5. In another shallow bowl, mix remaining ½ cup of flour, Italian breadcrumbs, seasoned salt, garlic salt, and black pepper.
6. Dip floured mushroom in egg and then coat with breadcrumb mixture.
7. When the temperature indicator light has turned off, fry mushrooms for about 3-5 minutes or until golden brown.
8. With a slotted spoon, transfer the mushrooms onto a paper towel-lined plate to drain.
9. Serve immediately.

BANANA PEPPERS

I don't usually even like banana peppers, but these are delicious! They are perfect for dressing up burgers or bratwursts and even taste great served up by themselves with your favorite dipping sauce. Frying them for 3-4 minutes is usually ideal, but keep a watchful eye so they don't burn.

Ingredients:

- ½ cup flour
- 1 teaspoon seasoned salt
- Ground black pepper, to taste
- 1 (16-ounce) jar banana pepper rings, drained

Preparation time: 10 minutes
Cooking time: 4 minutes

Directions:

1. Prepare fryer and set the temperature to 356 degrees. Cover the fryer with the lid.
2. In a large bowl, mix together flour, seasoned salt, and black pepper. Add banana pepper rings and gently toss to coat.
3. When the temperature indicator light has turned off, fry pepper rings for about 3-4 minutes or until golden brown.
4. With a slotted spoon, transfer the pepper rings onto a paper towel-lined plate to drain.
5. Serve immediately.

CRISPY DEVILED EGGS

This is a perfect party appetizer with a fresh take on traditional deviled eggs. Frying the eggs gives them just the right amount of crispiness, while the yellow center stays creamy, almost melting in your mouth. Your guests are sure to be impressed when you serve this one.

Ingredients:

- 12 whole eggs
- ¼ cup mayonnaise
- 1 tablespoon fresh chives, chopped
- 1 teaspoon lemon zest
- 1 tablespoon Dijon mustard
- Dash of hot sauce
- Salt and freshly ground black pepper, to taste
- 1 cup all-purpose flour
- 2 eggs, beaten
- 1 cup panko breadcrumbs
- Fresh parsley, chopped, for garnishing

Preparation time: **20** *minutes*
Cooking time: **8** *minutes*

Directions:

1. In a large pan, place eggs and enough cold water to cover and bring to a boil. Remove from heat and set aside for about 14 minutes.
2. Prepare fryer and set the temperature to 356 degrees. Cover the fryer with the lid.
3. Drain the eggs completely. Peel eggs and cut in half lengthwise.
4. Remove yolks and transfer into a bowl. Add mayonnaise, chives, lemon zest, mustard, hot sauce, salt, and black pepper. With a wooden spoon, mash yolks until well combined.
5. Fill egg white halves with egg yolk mixture evenly.
6. In a shallow bowl, mix together flour, salt, and black pepper. In a second shallow bowl, beat eggs. In a third shallow bowl, place panko breadcrumbs.
7. Carefully coat eggs with flour mixture and then dip in egg. Finally, coat eggs with breadcrumbs.
8. When the temperature indicator light has turned off, fry eggs for about 1-2 minutes per side or until golden brown.
9. With a slotted spoon, transfer the eggs onto a paper towel-lined plate to drain.
10. Serve immediately with a garnish of parsley.

BUFFALO CHICKEN RANGOON

This appetizer contains the perfect packaging of the fried wonton wrapper housing a delicious creamy buffalo chicken stuffing. It is a great recipe to serve up on game day with a side of blue cheese or ranch dressing and maybe a few carrot and celery sticks.

Ingredients:

- 1 boneless chicken breast
- 8 ounces cream cheese, softened
- ½ cup buffalo sauce
- 1 teaspoon onion powder
- 1 teaspoon garlic powder
- 1 (12-ounce) package wonton wrappers

Preparation time: 15 minutes
Cooking time: 8 minutes

Directions:

1. Prepare fryer and set the temperature to 356 degrees. Cover the fryer with the lid.
2. In a pan of boiling water, add chicken breast over medium heat and cook, covered, for about 15-17 minutes. Drain chicken and shred with a fork.
3. In a bowl, add chicken, cream cheese, buffalo sauce, garlic powder, and onion powder and mix until well combined.
4. Spread wrappers out on a smooth surface.
5. Place a heaping tablespoon of chicken filling in the center of each wrapper. With your fingers, slightly moisten the edges of the wrapper with water. Fold the wrapper in a triangle shape and press to seal.
6. Pull right and left corners up, attaching them to seal on top.
7. Repeat with remaining wrappers and filling mixture.
8. When the temperature indicator light has turned off, fry dumplings for about 1-2 minutes or until golden brown on all sides.
9. With a slotted spoon, transfer the dumplings onto a paper towel-lined plate to drain.
10. Serve immediately.

PICKLES WITH TANGY DIP

The first time I had fried pickles was at a little basement bar while on vacation, and I'll admit I was a bit skeptical. I like pickles okay, but I wasn't sure about them starring as the whole appetizer. After one bite, I was sold! Breading and frying the pickle is the perfect complement to their tangy taste and a good dipping sauce goes a long way. You'll enjoy frying these up in your own deep fryer.

Ingredients:

For Dip:

- ¼ cup mayonnaise
- 1 tablespoon ketchup
- 1 tablespoon horseradish
- ¼ teaspoon Cajun seasoning

For Pickles:

- ¼ cup flour
- ¼ teaspoon dried basil, crushed
- ¼ teaspoon dried oregano, crushed
- 1 teaspoon Cajun seasoning
- 1/8 teaspoon cayenne pepper
- Kosher salt, to taste
- 2 cups dill pickles, drained and sliced

Preparation time: 15 minutes
Cooking time: 3 minutes

Directions:

1. Prepare fryer and set the temperature to 374 degrees. Cover the fryer with the lid.
2. For dip: In a bowl, add all ingredients and mix until well combined. Refrigerate until serving.
3. For pickles: In a bowl, mix together flour, herbs, Cajun seasoning, cayenne pepper, and salt.
4. Coat pickles with flour mixture evenly and shake off excess.
5. When the temperature indicator light has turned off, fry pickles for about 2-3 minutes or until golden brown.
6. With a slotted spoon, transfer the pickles onto a paper towel-lined plate to drain.
7. Serve immediately alongside dip.

MOZZARELLA STICKS

Cheesy mozzarella sticks are a perfect appetizer or snack when hunger strikes. These sticks use pre-packaged string cheese, so they couldn't be easier to put together. Keep a close eye on them while they're frying as you don't want the cheese to come bubbling out the sides.

Ingredients:

- 2 eggs
- 2 tablespoons milk
- 1½ cups Italian breadcrumbs
- 16 ounces string cheese
- Marinara sauce, for dipping

Preparation time: *10 minutes*
Cooking time: *1 minutes*

Directions:

1. Prepare fryer and set the temperature to 374 degrees. Cover the fryer with the lid.
2. In a shallow bowl, add eggs and milk and beat until well combined.
3. In another shallow bowl, place breadcrumbs.
4. Dip string cheese in egg mixture evenly and then coat with breadcrumbs. Repeat coating process once more.
5. When the temperature indicator light has turned off, fry cheese sticks for about 1 minute or until golden brown.
6. With a slotted spoon, transfer the cheese sticks onto a paper towel-lined plate to drain.
7. Serve immediately alongside marinara dipping sauce.

JALAPEÑO POPPERS

Cheesy jalapeño poppers have been a long time deep fryer favorite, especially to those who like things a little spicy. They are pretty easy to whip up in your own kitchen; just use caution when handling those jalapeños. I recommend using gloves and be sure not to touch around your eyes.

Ingredients:

- 1 cup Mexican cheese blend, shredded
- 8 ounces cream cheese, softened
- 1 teaspoon Cajun seasoning
- 1 cup whole milk
- 2 cups flour
- 2 cups plain breadcrumbs
- 12 whole jalapeño peppers, halved lengthwise and seeded

Preparation time: 15 minutes
Cooking time: 3 minutes

Directions:

1. Prepare fryer and set the temperature to 374 degrees. Cover the fryer with the lid.
2. In a bowl, mix Mexican cheese, cream cheese, and Cajun seasoning. Spoon cheese mixture in pepper halves evenly.
3. In a shallow bowl, place milk. In a second shallow bowl, place flour. In a third shallow bowl, place breadcrumbs.
4. Dip peppers in milk and then coat with flour. Again, dip in milk and then coat with breadcrumbs. Again, dip in milk and then coat with breadcrumbs a second time.
5. When the temperature indicator light has turned off, fry peppers for about 2-3 minutes or until golden brown.
6. With a slotted spoon, transfer the peppers onto a paper towel-lined plate to drain.
7. Serve immediately.

POPCORN SHRIMP

Bite sized shrimp in perfectly seasoned breading make this dish a great snack. Mix up some cocktail sauce and enjoy.

Ingredients:

- 1 cup all-purpose flour
- ½ cup milk
- 1 egg
- 1 cup dry breadcrumbs
- ½ teaspoon dried parsley, crushed
- ½ teaspoon dried basil, crushed
- 1/8 teaspoon onion powder
- 1/8 teaspoon garlic powder
- Salt, to taste
- 24 uncooked medium shrimp, peeled and deveined

Preparation time: 20 minutes
Cooking time: 4 minutes

Directions:

1. Prepare fryer and set the temperature to 338 degrees. Cover the fryer with the lid.
2. In a shallow bowl, place flour. In a second shallow bowl, add milk and egg and beat until well combined. Use a third shallow bowl to mix together breadcrumbs, herbs, onion powder, garlic powder, and salt.
3. Coat shrimp with flour and shake off excess. Dip shrimp into egg mixture and then coat with bread crumbs. Gently shake off excess bread crumbs.
4. When the temperature indicator light has turned off, fry shrimp for about 3-4 minutes or until golden brown on all sides.
5. With a slotted spoon, transfer the shrimp onto a paper towel-lined plate to drain.
6. Serve immediately.

BLOOMIN' ONION & DIPPING SAUCE

I don't know that there is a more perfect appetizer than the bloomin' onion. It has a nice presentation, there's plenty for everyone, and it's so good. Now you don't have to go out to a restaurant to enjoy one of these. It does take a little practice learning the cutting technique, so plan to practice on a few onions before frying. Just be sure to only cut about 3/4 of the way down, so the onion will be held together.

Ingredients:

For Dipping Sauce:

- ½ cup mayonnaise
- 2 tablespoons cream-style horseradish sauce
- 2 tablespoons ketchup
- 1 teaspoon paprika
- ¼ teaspoon cayenne pepper
- ¼ teaspoon salt
- ⅛ teaspoon ground black pepper

For Onion Rings:

- 1 large sweet onion
- 4 eggs
- 2 cups flour
- 2 teaspoons paprika
- 1 teaspoon cayenne pepper
- ½ teaspoon ground cumin
- Salt and freshly ground black pepper, to taste

> Preparation time: 20 minutes
> Cooking time: 10 minutes

Directions:

1. Prepare fryer and set the temperature to 356 degrees. Cover the fryer with the lid.
2. For sauce: In a bowl, add all ingredients and mix until well combined. Refrigerate until serving.
3. With a narrow knife, carefully remove the center of the onion. With a very sharp knife, slice onion several times to create petals about ¾ of the way down. Cut the onion into 90 degrees to have 16 sections or petals and then gently spread petals apart.
4. In a deep bowl, beat eggs.
5. In another deep bowl, mix together flour and spices, salt, and pepper.
6. Dip onion in eggs and then coat with flour mixture. You may need to spoon the mixture over the onion to help coat entirely. Repeat this coating process once more.
7. When the temperature indicator light has turned off, fry onion for about 10 minutes or until golden brown on all sides.
8. With a slotted spoon, transfer the bloomin' onion onto a paper towel-lined plate to drain.
9. Serve immediately.

CHINESE EGG ROLLS

These delicious egg rolls are authentic and take a little time to prepare, but they are definitely worth it. It makes quite a large batch, but they can be frozen and reheated. Be sure the vegetables are very dry or you will have soggy egg rolls. Serve with your favorite dipping sauce, such as sweet and sour or duck sauce.

Ingredients:

- 8 cups green cabbage, shredded
- 8 cups savoy cabbage, shredded
- 2 cups celery, shredded
- 2 cups carrot, peeled and shredded
- 3 cups roast pork, shredded
- 2 cups cooked shrimp, chopped
- 3 scallions, chopped
- 2 tablespoons vegetable oil
- 1 tablespoon sesame oil
- 2 teaspoons sugar
- ¼ teaspoon five-spice powder
- 2½ teaspoons salt
- ¼ teaspoon ground white pepper
- 24 egg roll wrappers
- 1 egg, beaten

Preparation time: 25 minutes
Cooking time: 7 minutes

Directions:

1. Prepare fryer and set the temperature to 320 degrees. Cover the fryer with the lid.
2. In a large pan of boiling water, cook cabbage, celery, and carrots for about 2 minutes.
3. Drain vegetables and transfer into an ice bath for a few minutes. Drain vegetables and squeeze out all moisture completely. With kitchen towel, pat vegetables dry.
4. In a large bowl, add vegetables and remaining ingredients except wrappers and egg and toss to coat well.
5. Spread wrappers out on a smooth surface.
6. Place desired amount of filling onto each wrapper in a log shape and fold one corner up over one long side of the filling. Brush the corners of the wrapper lightly with the beaten egg. Fold left and right (end) corners toward the center and continue to roll. Repeat with remaining filling and wrappers.
7. When the temperature indicator light has turned off, fry rolls for about 5 minutes or until golden brown on all sides.
8. With a slotted spoon, transfer the rolls onto a paper towel-lined plate to drain.
9. Serve immediately.

BACON, CHICKEN & CHEESE ROLLS

These cheesy chicken balls are a perfect appetizer to serve at any event. They look fancy enough to be served individually with toothpicks at a more elegant occasion, but are filled with delicious favorites that everyone is sure to love just sitting around on game day. Add enough mayonnaise so that the ingredients just stick together. You don't want to add too much and have the balls become soggy.

Ingredients:

- 1 medium-sized chicken breast, shredded
- 3 bacon slices, cooked and diced
- ½ cup parmesan cheese, grated
- 1 tablespoon mayonnaise, more if mixture is too dry
- ½ teaspoon dried parsley, crushed
- 3 teaspoons all-purpose flour
- Salt and freshly ground black pepper, to taste
- ¾ cup breadcrumbs

Preparation time: *15 minutes*
Cooking time: *10 minutes*

Directions:

1. Prepare fryer and set the temperature to 356 degrees. Cover the fryer with the lid.
2. In a bowl, add all ingredients except breadcrumbs and mix until well combined.
3. Make 1-inch balls from chicken mixture. Coat balls with breadcrumbs evenly.
4. When the temperature indicator light has turned off, fry chicken balls for about 10 minutes or until golden brown on all sides.
5. With a slotted spoon, transfer the chicken balls onto a paper towel-lined plate to drain.
6. Serve immediately.

Main Courses
Poultry

CHICKEN WITH MILK GRAVY

Fried chicken is a southern staple, especially when served up with a delicious gravy. This is a simple gravy to make. You can enhance the flavor by using any variety of spices you enjoy. I sometimes add just a hint of extra pepper.

Ingredients:

- 6-8 bone-in, skin-on chicken breasts, each cut into 2 pieces
- 1-2 cups buttermilk
- Salt and freshly ground black pepper, to taste
- 2 cups all-purpose flour
- 1 teaspoon dried thyme, crushed
- 1 teaspoon paprika
- ½ teaspoon cayenne pepper
- 1 teaspoon garlic powder
- 1 teaspoon ground white pepper
- ¼ cup hot sauce
- 2 eggs
- 3 cups milk

Directions:

1. In a large bowl, place chicken pieces and pour buttermilk over top to cover.
2. Refrigerate to marinate for about 4-6 hours or overnight.
3. Prepare fryer and set the temperature to 356 degrees. Cover the fryer with the lid.
4. Drain chicken completely and season lightly with salt and black pepper.
5. In a shallow bowl, mix together flour, thyme, paprika, cayenne pepper, garlic powder, salt, white pepper, and black pepper.
6. Reserve ¼ cup of flour mixture for gravy.
7. In another shallow bowl, add hot sauce and eggs and beat well.
8. Coat chicken pieces with flour and shake off any excess. Then, dip chicken pieces in egg mixture and shake off any excess. Again, coat chicken pieces with flour mixture and shake off any excess.
9. When the temperature indicator light has turned off, fry chicken pieces until golden brown on all sides.
10. With a slotted spoon, transfer the chicken pieces onto a paper towel-lined plate to drain.
11. Transfer ¼ cup of oil from fryer into a pan over medium heat.
12. Stir in reserved flour mixture and cook for about 2-3 minutes stirring continuously.
13. Slowly add milk, beating continuously until smooth.
14. Cook until gravy becomes thick and smooth.
15. Serve chicken pieces with the topping of milk gravy.

Preparation time: 15 minutes
Cooking time: 15 minutes

BEER BATTERED CHICKEN NUGGETS

These nuggets will be loved by both kids and adults. Don't worry about serving these to the little ones, the alcohol burns off during the cooking process, and leaves the nuggets tender and flavorful. Serve with a big side of ketchup, barbecue, honey mustard, or whatever your favorite dipping sauce might be.

Ingredients:

- 2 skinless, boneless chicken breasts, cut into bite-sized nugget pieces
- 1 cup all-purpose flour
- ¼ teaspoon salt
- 1 cup beer
- ½ cup water
- 1 egg

Preparation time: 15 minutes
Cooking time: 5 minutes

Directions:

1. Prepare fryer and set the temperature to 338 degrees. Cover the fryer with the lid.
2. In a bowl, mix together flour and salt. Add beer and stir to combine. Add water and beat until smooth. Add egg and beat until a smooth mixture is formed.
3. Coat chicken nuggets with beer mixture evenly.
4. When the temperature indicator light has turned off, fry nuggets for about 2-5 minutes or until golden brown on all sides.
5. With a slotted spoon, transfer the nuggets onto a paper towel-lined plate to drain.
6. Serve immediately.

NASHVILLE HOT CHICKEN

I just love the town of Nashville and lately people can't get enough of Nashville's hot chicken, a preparation for frying and coating chicken in a cayenne pepper sauce. This stuff is spicy! Lines are out the door at all of the Nashville hot spots, but you can create it in your own kitchen using your deep fryer. Just be sure to serve it up Nashville style with a slice of white bread and a side of pickles.

Ingredients:

- 2 (3½-4 pound) chickens, each cut into 10 pieces
- 2 tablespoons plus 4 teaspoons kosher salt
- 1 tablespoon freshly ground black pepper
- 4 cups all-purpose flour
- 2 cups buttermilk
- 4 large eggs
- 2 tablespoons Tabasco sauce
- 2 tablespoons dark brown sugar
- 6 tablespoons cayenne pepper
- 1 teaspoon paprika
- 1 teaspoon chili powder
- 1 teaspoon garlic powder

Preparation time: 15 minutes
Cooking time: 18 minutes

Directions:

1. Season chicken with 2 tablespoons of salt and 1 tablespoon black pepper and place into a large bowl. Refrigerate, covered, for at least 3 hours.
2. Prepare fryer and set the temperature to 356 degrees. Cover the fryer with the lid.
3. In a large, shallow bowl, mix together flour and remaining 4 teaspoons of salt.
4. In another large shallow bowl, add buttermilk, eggs, and hot sauce and beat well.
5. With paper towels, pat dry chicken pieces.
6. Coat chicken pieces with flour mixture, shaking off excess. Now, dip in egg mixture and again coat with flour mixture.
7. When the temperature indicator light has turned off, fry chicken pieces for about 15-18 minutes or until golden brown on all sides.
8. With a slotted spoon, transfer the chicken pieces onto a paper towel-lined plate to drain.
9. Transfer 1 cup of oil from fryer into a heatproof bowl and set aside to cool.
10. After oil is cooled, add brown sugar and spices and beat until well combined.
11. Coat fried chicken pieces with spicy oil evenly and serve.

CHIPOTLE HONEY CHICKEN CRISPERS

These chicken tenders are extra crispy and served smothered in a sauce that has a delicious spicy kick. By coating the chicken tenders in both a liquid coating and then again in a flour breading, the pieces become extra crispy in the fryer.

Ingredients:

For Sauce:

- 2/3 cup honey
- ¼ cup ketchup
- ¼ cup water
- 1 tablespoon apple cider vinegar
- ½ teaspoon hot sauce
- 1-2 teaspoons chipotle chili powder
- ½ teaspoon salt

For Dipping Mixture:

- ½ cup chicken broth
- ½ cup milk
- 1 egg
- ¼ teaspoon garlic powder
- 1¼ teaspoons salt
- ¼ teaspoon pepper
- ¾ cup flour

For Coating Mixture:

- 1½ cups flour
- 1 teaspoon paprika
- ½ teaspoon garlic powder
- 1 teaspoon salt
- ½ teaspoon black pepper

For Chicken:

- 12 chicken tenderloins

Directions:

1. Prepare fryer and set the temperature to 356 degrees. Cover the fryer with the lid.
2. For sauce: In a small pan, add all ingredients and bring to a gentle boil, stirring continuously. Cook for about 2 minutes, stirring continuously. Remove from heat and transfer into a bowl. Set aside until using.
3. For dipping mixture: In a shallow bowl, add all ingredients except flour and beat until well combined. Add flour and beat until smooth.
4. For coating mixture: In another shallow bowl, mix together all ingredients.
5. Dip chicken tenderloins in milk mixture evenly and then coat with flour mixture.
6. When the temperature indicator light has turned off, fry chicken tenderloins for about 4 minutes or until golden brown.
7. With a slotted spoon, transfer the chicken tenderloins onto a paper towel-lined plate to drain.
8. Transfer chicken tenderloins into the bowl of sauce and toss to coat well.
9. Serve immediately.

Preparation time: *15 minutes*
Cooking time: *9 minutes*

COCONUT CHICKEN STRIPS

These coconut chicken strips are delightfully sweet, with just a hint of spice. They are delicious served all by themselves or with a side of mango salsa for dipping.

Ingredients:

- ¼ cup milk
- 2 eggs
- 1 tablespoon Sriracha sauce
- 1½ cups sweetened flaked coconut
- ¾ cup panko breadcrumbs
- ¼ teaspoon cayenne
- 1 teaspoon kosher salt
- ½ teaspoon freshly ground black pepper
- 1½ pound boneless chicken breasts, cut into strips

Preparation time: **15** *minutes*
Cooking time: **8** *minutes*

Directions:

1. Prepare fryer and set the temperature to 374 degrees. Cover the fryer with the lid.
2. In a shallow bowl, add the milk, eggs, and Sriracha sauce and beat until well combined
3. In another shallow dish mix together coconut, panko, cayenne, salt, and pepper.
4. Dip chicken strips in egg mixture and then coat with coconut mixture evenly.
5. When the temperature indicator light has turned off, fry chicken strips for about 3-4 minutes per side or until golden brown.
6. With a slotted spoon, transfer the chicken strips onto a paper towel-lined plate to drain.
7. Serve immediately.

CAJUN CHICKEN

Did you know that marinating your chicken in buttermilk adds both flavor and helps to tenderize the meat? For this Cajun fried chicken recipe, it's important to marinate the meat for at least 2 hours, preferably overnight. This chicken has the perfect crunch and just the right amount of spice.

Ingredients:

- 2 pounds bone-in chicken pieces
- 4 cups buttermilk
- Garlic powder, to taste
- Kosher salt and freshly ground black pepper, to taste
- 4 cups all-purpose flour
- 1 tablespoon cayenne pepper
- 2 teaspoons paprika
- 3 large eggs
- 1/3 cup water
- 1 cup hot sauce

Preparation time: 15 minutes
Cooking time: 18 minutes

Directions:

1. In a large bowl, place chicken pieces and pour buttermilk over top to cover.
2. Marinate in the refrigerator for at least 2 hours or up to overnight.
3. Remove the chicken pieces from buttermilk and sprinkle with garlic powder, salt, and black pepper.
4. In a shallow bowl, mix together flour, cayenne pepper, paprika, salt, and black pepper.
5. In another shallow bowl, add eggs, water, and hot sauce and beat well.
6. Coat chicken pieces with flour mixture and then coat with egg mixture. Dip again in flour mixture, shaking off any excess flour.
7. Arrange chicken pieces onto a baking sheet and refrigerate for about 30 minutes.
8. Prepare fryer and set the temperature to 356 degrees. Cover the fryer with the lid.
9. When the temperature indicator light has turned off, fry chicken for about 15-18 minutes or until golden brown.
10. Using tongs, transfer the chicken onto a paper towel-lined plate to drain.
11. Serve immediately.

CHICKEN POT PIE POCKETS

Chicken pot pies are a guilty pleasure of mine and, while the pre-packaged frozen variety is fine, nothing tastes better than homemade. And if you want to take it to the next level, you mix it up with an easy to transport, crispy pocket and suddenly you have magic. Your whole family will love this for dinner or a filling snack.

Ingredients:

- ¾ cup unsalted butter, divided
- ½ small yellow onion, chopped
- 1/3 cup all-purpose flour
- ¼ teaspoon dried thyme, crushed
- ½ teaspoon salt
- ¼ teaspoon ground black pepper
- 1¾ cups chicken broth
- ½ cup milk
- 2½ cups rotisserie chicken meat, shredded
- 10 ounces frozen mixed vegetables (peas, carrots, corn), thawed
- 16 frozen empanada wrappers, thawed

Preparation time: 15 minutes
Cooking time: 10 minutes

Directions:

1. Prepare fryer and set the temperature to 338 degrees. Cover the fryer with the lid.
2. In a large pan, melt ½ cup of butter over medium heat and sauté onion for about 2 minutes. Add flour, thyme, salt, and black pepper and stir until well combined. Slowly add broth and milk, stirring continuously. Cook for about 2 minutes, stirring often. Stir in chicken and vegetables and remove from heat.
3. Spread empanada wrappers out on a lightly floured surface. With a wet finger, moisten the edges of the wrappers. Place about ½ cup of chicken mixture in the center of 8 of the wrappers. Place remaining 8 wrappers on top of the filling, moist edges down. With the tines of a fork, crimp the edges to seal.
4. When the temperature indicator light has turned off, fry pie pockets for about 2-3 minutes per side or until golden brown.
5. With a slotted spoon, transfer the pie pockets onto a paper towel-lined plate to drain.
6. In a small microwave-safe dish, add remaining ¼ cup of butter and microwave until melted. Immediately brush both sides of pie pockets with melted butter and serve.

BUFFALO CHICKEN WINGS

Who needs to go out for wings when you can fry up a batch with your T-Fal in no time at all? These spicy wings will impress everyone at your table. Serve with ranch, blue cheese, and some celery and carrots. Booyah!

Ingredients:

- 1 cup flour
- 1½ teaspoons garlic powder
- 1 tablespoon paprika
- 1 teaspoon cayenne pepper
- Salt and freshly ground black pepper, to taste
- 3 pounds chicken wings
- ½ cup salted butter
- 1 cup buffalo sauce
- 3 tablespoons honey

Preparation time: 15 minutes
Cooking time: 20 minutes

Directions:

1. In a large shallow bowl, mix together flour, garlic powder, paprika, cayenne pepper, salt, and black pepper to taste.
2. Add chicken wings and generously coat with flour mixture.
3. Arrange chicken pieces onto a baking sheet and refrigerate for about 30 minutes.
4. Prepare fryer and set the temperature to 356 degrees. Cover the fryer with the lid.
5. When the temperature indicator light has turned off, fry chicken wings for about 10-15 minutes or until golden brown.
6. Meanwhile, in a pan, melt butter over medium-high heat. Add buffalo sauce and honey and bring to a boil, stirring continuously. Reduce the heat and simmer for about 10-15 minutes.
7. Transfer sauce into a large heatproof bowl.
8. With a slotted spoon, transfer wings onto a paper towel-lined plate to drain.
9. Add wings to sauce and toss to coat well.
10. Serve immediately.

STICKY GARLIC CHICKEN WINGS

Chicken wings may be thought of as the ultimate game day appetizer, but they are delicious any time. I know my crew loves to put 'em away for dinner. These are easy to prepare and are served in a sauce that everyone will love. Be sure to have plenty of napkins around the table for this messy feast!

Ingredients:

For Glaze:

- 2 tablespoons olive oil
- 5 garlic cloves, minced
- 1 cup honey
- ¼ cup soy sauce
- 1 teaspoon black pepper

For Chicken:

- 2 cups flour
- 5 tablespoons ground ginger
- 2 teaspoons cayenne pepper
- 1½ tablespoon salt
- 2 teaspoons ground black pepper
- 2 eggs
- 3 tablespoons cold water
- 3 pounds chicken wings

Preparation time: 15 minutes
Cooking time: 32 minutes

Directions:

1. Prepare fryer and set the temperature to 356 degrees. Cover the fryer with the lid.
2. For glaze: In a small pan, heat oil over medium heat and sauté garlic for about 1 minute. Add honey, soy sauce, and black pepper and simmer for about 10 minutes, stirring occasionally. Remove from heat and transfer into a heatproof bowl. Set aside until using.
3. For chicken: In a large, shallow bowl, mix together flour, ginger, cayenne pepper, salt, and black pepper.
4. In another shallow bowl, add eggs and cold water and beat until well combined.
5. Dip chicken wings into egg mixture and then coat with flour mixture.
6. When the temperature indicator light has turned off, fry chicken wings for about 15-20 minutes or until golden brown.
7. With a slotted spoon, transfer the chicken wings onto a paper towel-lined plate to drain.
8. Immediately add wings to the bowl of glaze and stir to combine.
9. Serve immediately.

CRISPY CHICKEN GIZZARDS

Chicken gizzards are a surprisingly popular dish to eat throughout the world. There is a town in Michigan that even hosts an annual Gizzard Fest with of course…a gizzard-eating contest. Here in the South, gizzards are typically fried and served with your favorite dipping sauce.

Ingredients:

- 1 cup whole buttermilk
- 2 tablespoons hot sauce
- 3 teaspoons seasoning salt, divided
- 1 pound chicken gizzards, cleaned
- 1 cup self-rising flour
- 2 teaspoons smoked paprika
- Freshly ground black pepper, to taste

Preparation time: 15 minutes
Cooking time: 6 minutes

Directions:

1. In a large bowl, mix together buttermilk, hot sauce, and 2 teaspoons of seasoning salt. Add chicken gizzards and coat with buttermilk mixture generously.
2. Marinate in refrigerator for 8 hours to overnight.
3. Prepare fryer and set the temperature to 320 degrees. Cover the fryer with the lid.
4. In a shallow bowl, mix together flour, remaining teaspoon of seasoning salt, paprika, and black pepper.
5. Drain chicken gizzards and coat with flour mixture evenly.
6. When the temperature indicator light has turned off, fry chicken gizzards for about 4-6 minutes or until golden brown.
7. With a slotted spoon, transfer chicken gizzards onto a paper towel-lined plate to drain.
8. Serve immediately.

GENERAL TSO'S CHICKEN

General Tso's is one of my absolute favorite Chinese food take-out dishes. The crunchy chicken in the sticky, slightly spicy sauce just can't be beat. Making it in my own kitchen is super easy…and delicious. To make it authentic, try to find some chopsticks. Serve over rice with a side of broccoli.

Ingredients:

For Marinade:

- 2 large eggs whites
- 2 tablespoons dark soy sauce
- 1 tablespoon Chinese rice wine
- 1½ pounds boneless, skinless chicken breasts, cut into ½ inch pieces

For Coating:

- ¾ cup cornstarch
- ¼ cup all-purpose flour
- ½ teaspoon baking powder
- ½ teaspoon salt

For Sauce:

- ½ cup chicken broth
- 3 tablespoons soy sauce
- 2 tablespoons Chinese rice vinegar
- 2 tablespoons Chinese rice wine
- 2 teaspoons sesame oil
- 3 tablespoons white granulated sugar
- 2 teaspoons cornstarch
- 1 tablespoon cooking oil
- 6 small dried red chilies, seeded and broken into pieces
- 2 teaspoons fresh ginger, minced
- 2 large garlic cloves, minced
- 3 scallions, cut into 1 inch pieces

Directions:

1. Prepare fryer and set the temperature to 374 degrees. Cover the fryer with the lid.
2. For marinade: In a bowl, add all ingredients except chicken and mix until well combined. Add chicken and coat with marinade generously. Set aside until using.
3. For coating: In a bowl, mix together all ingredients.
4. For sauce: In a bowl, add broth, soy sauce, vinegar, rice wine, sesame oil, sugar, and cornstarch and mix until sugar and cornstarch are dissolved.
5. Remove chicken pieces from marinade and shake off the excess.
6. Coat chicken pieces with flour mixture, shaking off the excess.
7. When the temperature indicator light has turned off, fry chicken pieces for about 3-4 minutes or until golden brown.
8. With a slotted spoon, transfer chicken pieces onto a paper towel-lined plate to drain.
9. For sauce: In a large skillet, heat cooking oil over medium-high heat and sauté red chilies, ginger, and garlic for about 30 seconds.
10. Add broth mixture and simmer until sauce becomes thick.
11. Stir in fried chicken and simmer for about 1 minute.
12. Stir in scallions and serve immediately.

Preparation time: *15 minutes*
Cooking time: *10 minutes*

TURKEY BREAST

While a whole turkey won't fit in your T-Fal fryer, a turkey breast will and it is every bit as delicious and simple. This turkey breast is a great meal, even if it's not Thanksgiving. The T-Fal makes it so easy to fry a turkey for your family, even if it's a busy week night.

Ingredients:

- 1 (3-3½-pound) turkey breast
- 3 tablespoons Cajun seasoning

Preparation time: 15 minutes
Cooking time: 17 minutes

Directions:

1. With paper towels, pat turkey breast dry.
2. Coat chicken breast with Cajun seasoning generously.
3. With plastic wrap, cover the breast and set aside for about 15-20 minutes.
4. Prepare fryer and set the temperature to 356 degrees. Cover the fryer with the lid.
5. When the temperature indicator light has turned off, fry turkey breast for about 15-17 minutes or until golden brown.
6. With a slotted spoon, transfer turkey breast onto a paper towel-lined plate to drain for about 5-7 minutes.
7. Cut into ½-inch slices and serve.

TURKEY LEGS

I like to use the T-Fal to deep fry some turkey legs to serve at our annual Thanksgiving dinner. I usually have the whole family over, sometime 35-40 people, so we always have plenty of food and several turkeys. Sadly, there are rarely leftovers of these turkey legs. Everyone enjoys them and I know your family will, too.

Ingredients:

- 4 cups buttermilk
- 2 tablespoons onion powder, divided
- 2 tablespoons garlic powder, divided
- 2 tablespoons paprika, divided
- 2 teaspoons cayenne pepper, divided
- Kosher salt and freshly ground black pepper, to taste
- 6 turkey drumsticks
- 2 cups all-purpose flour

Preparation time: 15 minutes
Cooking time: 16 minutes

Directions:

1. In a large bowl, mix together buttermilk, 1 tablespoon each of onion powder, garlic powder, and paprika, 1 teaspoon of cayenne, salt, and black pepper to taste. Add turkey drumsticks and generously coat with marinade.
2. Refrigerate for at least 2 hours or up to overnight.
3. Prepare fryer and set the temperature to 374 degrees. Cover the fryer with the lid.
4. In a large shallow dish, mix together flour with remaining spices.
5. Remove turkey legs from marinade and pat dry with paper towels.
6. Coat turkey legs generously with flour mixture.
7. When the temperature indicator light has turned off, fry turkey legs for about 16 minutes or until golden brown.
8. With a slotted spoon, transfer turkey legs onto a paper towel-lined plate to drain.
9. Serve immediately.

THANKSGIVING FRITTERS

Our family loves a good fritter, and these were put together after we just couldn't bear to eat one more night of leftover turkey dinner. We got creative and now these fritters are requested every Saturday after Thanksgiving. Mix in whatever leftovers you have on hand. We've added peas and corn with delicious results.

Ingredients:

- 2 cups roasted turkey, shredded
- 1 cup prepared stuffing
- 1 cup mashed potatoes
- ½ cup onion, finely chopped
- 3 garlic cloves, minced
- ¾ ounce fresh Italian parsley leaves, finely chopped
- ¼ cup flour
- 1 egg, beaten
- ¼ teaspoon cayenne pepper
- Sea salt and freshly ground black pepper, to taste
- Cranberry sauce, for serving

Preparation time: 20 minutes
Cooking time: 8 minutes

Directions:

1. In a large bowl, add all ingredients except cranberry sauce and mix until well combined.
2. Make 8, ½-inch thick, equal-sized patties from mixture.
3. Arrange patties onto a baking sheet and refrigerate for about 30 minutes.
4. Prepare fryer and set the temperature to 374 degrees. Cover the fryer with the lid.
5. When the temperature indicator light has turned off, fry patties for about 4 minutes per side or until golden brown.
6. With a slotted spoon, transfer patties onto a paper towel-lined plate to drain.
7. Serve warm alongside cranberry sauce.

Seafood

SHRIMP

Fried shrimp is a particular favorite in my family. We always order it at restaurants when we are near the beach and the seafood is fresh. When we make our own fried shrimp at home, I like to look for the biggest shrimp I can find. These stay plump and juicy while they fry and don't dry out. Serve these shrimp with cocktail or tartar sauce.

Ingredients:

- 1 cup milk
- 1 egg
- 2 cups self-rising flour
- 1 teaspoon Cajun seasoning
- ½ teaspoon Old Bay seasoning
- 1 teaspoon lemon pepper
- 1 teaspoon kosher salt
- ¼ teaspoon freshly cracked black pepper
- 1 pound shrimp, peeled and deveined

Preparation time: 15 minutes
Cooking time: 4 minutes

Directions:

1. Prepare fryer and set the temperature to 356 degrees. Cover the fryer with the lid.
2. In a shallow bowl, add milk and egg and beat well.
3. In another large shallow bowl, mix together remaining ingredients, except shrimp.
4. With paper towels, pat shrimp completely dry.
5. Dip shrimp in egg mixture and then coat with flour mixture.
6. Again, repeat this dipping and coating process once more and then shake off any excess.
7. When the temperature indicator light has turned off, fry shrimp for about 3-4 minutes or until golden brown.
8. With a slotted spoon, transfer shrimp onto a paper towel-lined plate to drain.
9. Serve immediately.

COCONUT SHRIMP

Some of the most delicious coconut shrimp I've ever had were on my honeymoon and were served with a delicious fruity sauce that perfectly complemented the coconut flavor. Playing around with my fryer, this is the closest recipe I have found to that special meal. The sauce is easy to pull together and makes the shrimp quite special.

Ingredients:

- 1¼ cups cornstarch
- 1¼ cups all-purpose flour
- 6½ teaspoons baking powder
- ¼ teaspoon Cajun seasoning
- ½ teaspoon salt
- 1½ cups cold water
- ½ teaspoon canola oil
- 2½ cups sweetened shredded coconut
- 1 pound large shrimp, peeled and deveined
- 1 cup orange marmalade
- ¼ cup honey

Preparation time: 15 minutes
Cooking time: 5 minutes

Directions:

1. Prepare fryer and set the temperature to 374 degrees. Cover the fryer with the lid.
2. In a large shallow bowl, mix together cornstarch, flour, baking powder, Cajun seasoning, and salt.
3. Add water and oil and mix until smooth.
4. In another large shallow bowl, place coconut.
5. Dip shrimp in flour mixture and then coat with coconut.
6. When the temperature indicator light has turned off, fry shrimp for about 3 minutes or until golden brown.
7. With a slotted spoon, transfer shrimp onto a paper towel-lined plate to drain.
8. In a small pan, add marmalade and honey and cook until heated through, stirring continuously.
9. Serve shrimp with marmalade mixture.

CRISPY SHRIMP TEMPURA

The tempura batter for these shrimp is Japanese and is known for being quite crunchy. The key to producing this crunch is the temperature of both the batter and the oil used for frying. For the crunchiest batter, use ice cold water. Be careful not to over mix your batter, just mix until the ingredients are incorporated. The hot oil fries these shrimp quickly, producing a delicious crunchy texture you are sure to enjoy.

Ingredients:

- ½ cup rice wine
- ½ teaspoon salt, divided
- ½ pound shrimp, peeled and deveined
- ¼ cup all-purpose flour
- ¼ cup cornstarch
- 1/3 cup cold water
- 1 egg yolk
- 1 teaspoon shortening
- ½ teaspoon baking powder
- ¼ teaspoon white sugar

Preparation time: 15 minutes
Cooking time: 2 minutes

Directions:

1. In a bowl, mix together rice wine and ¼ teaspoon of salt.
2. Add shrimp, making sure they are covered by the wine.
3. Refrigerate, covered, for about 20-30 minutes.
4. Prepare fryer and set the temperature to 374 degrees. Cover the fryer with the lid.
5. Remove shrimp from refrigerator and use paper towels to pat dry.
6. In a bowl, add remaining ingredients and remaining ¼ teaspoon of salt and mix until just combined.
7. When the temperature indicator light has turned off, dip shrimp in the batter and add to the fryer. Fry shrimp for about 1½-2 minutes or until golden brown.
8. With a slotted spoon, transfer shrimp onto a paper towel-lined plate to drain.
9. Serve immediately.

BEER BATTERED COD

Cod is a simple white fish with mild flavor, so it is the perfect fish to beer batter and fry. The beer adds great flavor and keeps the batter light and crunchy. By adding just a teaspoon of hot sauce, you add taste without making it too spicy.

Ingredients:

- 1¼ cups all-purpose flour, divided
- ¼ cup white sugar
- 2 teaspoons baking powder
- Salt and freshly ground black pepper, to taste
- 2 eggs
- 1 teaspoon hot sauce
- 1 cup beer
- 2 pounds cod fillets, cut into strips

Preparation time: 15 minutes
Cooking time: 4 minutes

Directions:

1. Prepare fryer and set the temperature to 356 degrees. Cover the fryer with the lid.
2. In a large shallow bowl, place 1 cup of flour.
3. In another large shallow bowl, mix together remaining ¼ cup of flour, sugar, baking powder, salt, and pepper.
4. Add eggs and hot sauce and mix well.
5. Slowly add beer, stirring continuously until mixture becomes smooth.
6. Coat cod strips with flour and shake off any excess.
7. Then, dip cod strips in the beer batter.
8. When the temperature indicator light has turned off, fry cod strips for about 4 minutes or until golden brown.
9. With a slotted spoon, transfer cod strips onto a paper towel-lined plate to drain.
10. Serve immediately.

CRUNCHY BATTERED WHITEFISH

If you love your fried fish extra crispy and crunchy, then this is the batter for you. If you can't find cod, substitute with any flaky whitefish. Top it off by serving with a side of lemon and tartar sauce.

Ingredients:

- 2 pounds cod fillets, cut into 1½-inch strips
- 1¼ cups plus 2 tablespoons all-purpose flour, divided
- 1½ teaspoons paprika, divided
- 1 teaspoon garlic powder
- Salt and freshly ground black pepper, to taste
- 1 teaspoon baking powder
- ½ teaspoon baking soda
- 1-1½ cups cold water

Preparation time: *15 minutes*
Cooking time: *10 minutes*

Directions:

1. Prepare fryer and set the setting to 338 degrees. Cover the fryer with the lid.
2. In a sealable plastic bag, mix together 2 tablespoons of flour, 1 teaspoon of paprika, garlic powder, salt, and black pepper.
3. Add cod strips and seal the bag. Shake gently to coat well.
4. In a shallow bowl, mix together remaining 1¼ cups of flour, baking powder, baking soda, remaining ½ teaspoon of paprika, salt, and black pepper.
5. Add water and mix until a smooth mixture is formed.
6. Remove cod fillets from bag and coat with batter evenly.
7. When the temperature indicator light has turned off, fry fish for about 8-10 minutes or until golden brown flipping once to brown evenly. You will need to fry in batches as to not overcrowd your fryer.
8. With a slotted spoon, transfer the fish pieces to a paper towel-lined plate to drain.
9. Serve immediately.

SOUTHERN STYLE CATFISH

Fried catfish is a Southern classic, using both flour and cornmeal to give the batter an interesting texture and flavor. To make this a true Southern meal, be sure to also fry up some hush puppies on the side. Serve with coleslaw and dipping sauce of your choice.

Ingredients:

- 2 tablespoons Cajun seasoning
- 1 tablespoon onion powder
- 1 tablespoon garlic powder
- 1 tablespoon paprika
- Pinch of cayenne pepper
- 1 tablespoon black pepper
- 2 cups flour
- 2 cups cornmeal
- ½ cup hot sauce
- 2 eggs, beaten
- 2 tablespoons yellow mustard
- 10 catfish fillets, cut in half

Preparation time: 15 minutes
Cooking time: 5 minutes

Directions:

1. Prepare fryer and set the temperature to 338 degrees. Cover the fryer with the lid.
2. In a bowl, mix together the seasoning mixture of Cajun seasoning, onion powder, garlic powder, paprika, cayenne pepper, and black pepper.
3. In a large shallow bowl, mix together flour, cornmeal, and 2 tablespoons of seasoning mixture.
4. In another shallow bowl, add hot sauce, eggs, mustard, and remaining seasoning mixture and mix until well combined.
5. With paper towels, pat catfish pieces dry.
6. Coat catfish pieces with flour mixture and shake off any excess.
7. Then, dip catfish pieces into egg mixture. Add again to the flour mixture and shake to discard excess flour.
8. When the temperature indicator light has turned off, fry catfish pieces for about 4-5 minutes or until golden brown.
9. With a slotted spoon, transfer catfish pieces onto a paper towel-lined plate to drain.
10. Serve immediately.

SALT & PEPPER CALAMARI

Calamari is of course, squid, which means many people will shy away from eating it. And that's a shame because calamari is truly delicious. This makes a great appetizer or light meal with the simple salt and pepper fried coating that packs a surprising amount of flavor.

Ingredients:

- 2 egg whites
- 1/3 cup all-purpose flour
- ¼ cup cornstarch
- 1 teaspoon kosher salt
- 1 teaspoon freshly ground black pepper
- ¼ pound calamari rings, thawed

Preparation time: 15 minutes
Cooking time: 2 minutes

Directions:

1. Prepare fryer and set the temperature to 374 degrees. Cover the fryer with the lid.
2. In a shallow bowl, add egg whites and beat slightly.
3. In another shallow bowl, mix together flour, cornstarch, salt, and black pepper.
4. Dip calamari rings into egg whites evenly.
5. Then, coat with flour mixture and shake off any excess.
6. When the temperature indicator light has turned off, fry calamari rings for about 2 minutes or until golden brown.
7. With a slotted spoon, transfer calamari rings onto a paper towel-lined plate to drain.
8. Serve immediately.

BATTERED CLAMS

A hole-in-the-wall little seafood restaurant I used to go to served the most delicious fried clams. I'm not sure if it was because I loved the clams or the batter so much, but they were what I most frequently ordered. This is an easy recipe to fry up your own. Spritz with lemon, serve with tartar sauce, and enjoy.

Ingredients:

- ½ cup all-purpose flour
- ½ cup milk
- 1 tablespoon butter, melted and cooled
- 1 egg, separated
- ¼ teaspoon salt
- 2 cups shucked clams, rinsed and well-drained

Preparation time: 15 minutes
Cooking time: 1½ minutes

Directions:

1. Prepare fryer and set the temperature to 374 degrees. Cover the fryer with the lid.
2. In a bowl, add flour, milk, butter, egg yolk, and salt and beat until smooth.
3. In a small chilled bowl, add egg white and beat with an electric mixer until soft peaks form.
4. Fold the beaten egg white into the milk mixture.
5. With a fork, poke each clam and then dip into milk mixture evenly.
6. When the temperature indicator light has turned off, fry clams for about 1½ minutes or until golden brown.
7. With a slotted spoon, transfer clams onto a paper towel-lined plate to drain.
8. Serve immediately.

SOFT SHELL CRAB

Fried soft shell crab can be quite simple to cook. If you don't know how to clean the crabs yourself, just ask someone at your fish market to do it for you. For best results, fry these crabs within a few hours of them being cleaned.

Ingredients:

- 6 soft-shell crabs, rinsed
- 1½ teaspoons seasoned salt
- 1½ cups self-rising flour
- 1 (12-ounce) can evaporated milk
- 1 large egg
- ¼ cup water

Preparation time: 15 minutes
Cooking time: 3 minutes

Directions:

1. Prepare fryer and set the temperature to 374 degrees. Cover the fryer with the lid.
2. With paper towels, pat crabs dry and season with seasoned salt.
3. In a large shallow bowl, place flour.
4. In another large shallow bowl, add evaporated milk, egg, and water and beat until well combined.
5. Coat crabs with flour and then dip into egg mixture. Dredge in the flour once more, shaking off any excess.
6. When the temperature indicator light has turned off, fry crabs for about 2-3 minutes or until golden brown. Turn only once to brown evenly.
7. With a slotted spoon, transfer crabs onto a paper towel-lined plate to drain.
8. Serve immediately.

OYSTERS

I'm not one for eating oysters on the half shell, but serve me some fried oysters and I'll go to town on them. These oysters are delectable served with lemon wedges and hot sauce, or your favorite dipping sauce.

Ingredients:

- 20 medium fresh oysters, opened and removed from shells
- ½ cup bleached all-purpose flour plus more for dusting
- 2 tablespoons baking powder
- ¾ teaspoon salt
- 2 tablespoons peanut oil
- 1¼ cups cold water

Preparation time: 15 minutes
Cooking time: 4 minutes

Directions:

1. Prepare fryer and set the temperature to 374 degrees. Cover the fryer with the lid.
2. With paper towels, pat oysters dry and then dust with some flour.
3. In a bowl, add flour, baking powder, salt, oil, and water and mix until well combined.
4. Coat oysters with the batter evenly.
5. When the temperature indicator light has turned off, fry oysters for about 3-4 minutes or until golden brown.
6. With a slotted spoon, transfer oysters onto a paper towel-lined plate to drain.
7. Serve immediately.

OYSTER PO' BOY SANDWICH

The po' boy is a famous New Orleans-style sandwich filled with seafood and served on thick bread. This oyster po' boy is dressed with lettuce and a spicy mayo sauce that adds a lot of zest to the fried oysters. This recipe makes 4 large sandwiches, plenty for sharing.

Ingredients:

For Sauce:

- 1¼ cups mayonnaise
- ¼ cup stone-ground mustard
- 1 clove garlic, smashed
- 1 tablespoon capers
- 1 tablespoon pickle juice
- 1 teaspoon prepared horseradish
- ½ teaspoon hot sauce
- ¼ teaspoon hot paprika
- ¼ teaspoon cayenne pepper

For Oysters:

- 32 ounces shucked oysters
- 1 cup plus 1 tablespoon milk, divided
- 2 eggs
- 1 tablespoon water
- ¼ teaspoon cayenne pepper
- 1 cup all-purpose flour
- ½ cup cornmeal
- Kosher salt, to taste
- ½ teaspoon freshly ground black pepper

For Sandwich:

- 4 (6-inch) hoagie loaves, sliced horizontally
- 4 romaine lettuce leaves
- 1-2 lemons

Directions:

1. For sauce: In a food processor, add all ingredients and pulse until smooth.
2. Refrigerate to chill before serving.
3. For oysters: In a bowl, soak oysters in 1 cup of milk for about 15 minutes.
4. Prepare fryer and set the temperature to 356 degrees. Cover the fryer with the lid.
5. In a shallow bowl, add remaining 1 tablespoon of milk, eggs, water, and cayenne pepper.
6. In another shallow bowl, mix together flour, cornmeal, salt, and black pepper.
7. Drain milk from oysters completely.
8. Dip oysters in egg mixture and then coat with flour mixture.
9. When the temperature indicator light has turned off, fry oysters for about 3 minutes or until golden brown.
10. With a slotted spoon, transfer oysters onto a paper towel-lined plate to drain.
11. For sandwich: Spread sauce over inside of each loaf.
12. Arrange a lettuce leaf inside each loaf and top with oysters.
13. Squeeze fresh lemon juice over oysters and serve immediately.

Preparation time: 20 minutes
Cooking time: 3 minutes

CRAB FRITTERS WITH SPICY MAYO DIPPING SAUCE

This is a simple, but delightful meal that can be served to guests as either a main course or appetizer. The mayo dipping sauce is quite tasty. In fact, I've found myself whipping up the sauce to serve with other types of seafood. These fritters will go fast!

Ingredients:

- ¾ cup light mayonnaise
- 1 tablespoon prepared horseradish
- 1 tablespoon Dijon mustard
- 2 tablespoons fresh lemon juice
- 2 garlic cloves, peeled
- 1 tablespoon fresh chives, chopped
- 1 egg
- 1 cup hush puppy mix
- ½ cup milk
- 1 pound cooked lump crabmeat

Preparation time: 15 minutes
Cooking time: 15 minutes

Directions:

1. Prepare fryer and set the temperature to 374 degrees. Cover the fryer with the lid.
2. In a food processor, add mayonnaise, horseradish, mustard, lemon juice, and garlic and pulse until well combined.
3. Transfer mixture into a bowl.
4. Stir in chives and refrigerate, covered, until serving.
5. In a shallow bowl, add egg, hush puppy mix, and milk and mix until smooth.
6. Fold in crabmeat.
7. When the temperature indicator light has turned off, drop tablespoons of crab mixture and fry for about 2-3 minutes or until golden brown.
8. With a slotted spoon, transfer fritters onto a paper towel-lined plate to drain.
9. Serve immediately with mayonnaise sauce.

Pork, Beef, and Other Fun Stuff

SOUTHERN PORK CHOPS

These pork chops are so flavorful and easy, they are sure to become a weeknight staple. Season generously with salt and pepper, it will add plenty of flavor. Placing the chops in the refrigerator after coating them in flour ensures that the flour will stay on once the chops are added to the hot oil. Serve with a big helping of mashed potatoes and a green veggie.

Ingredients:

- 4 thin-cut bone-in pork chops
- Seasoned salt and freshly ground black pepper, to taste
- 1 cup buttermilk
- 1 cup self-rising flour

Preparation time: 15 minutes
Cooking time: 8 minutes

Directions:

1. Season pork chops with seasoned salt and black pepper evenly.
2. In a shallow bowl, add buttermilk.
3. In another shallow bowl, place flour.
4. Dip pork chops in buttermilk and then coat with flour evenly.
5. Arrange pork chops onto a plate and refrigerate for about 30 minutes.
6. Prepare fryer and set the temperature to 356 degrees. Cover the fryer with the lid.
7. When the temperature indicator light has turned off, fry pork chops for about 8 minutes or until golden brown, flipping once in the middle way.
8. With a slotted spoon, transfer pork chops onto a paper towel-lined plate to drain.
9. Serve immediately.

CHICKEN FRIED STEAK

Chicken fried steak uses cube steaks, which are pieces of beef that have been extra tenderized. This will make your chicken fried steak extra tender and delicious. I like to use the saltine crackers because I love the flavor but any salty cracker will do, even breadcrumbs in a pinch.

Ingredients:

- 4 cube steaks
- 2¼ teaspoons salt, divided
- 1¾ teaspoons ground black pepper, divided
- 1¼ cups all-purpose flour, divided
- 38 saltine crackers, crushed
- ½ teaspoon baking powder
- ½ teaspoon red chili powder
- 2 large eggs
- 4¾ cups milk, divided
- Chopped fresh parsley, for garnishing

Directions:

1. Prepare fryer and set the temperature to 356 degrees. Cover the fryer with the lid.
2. Season steak with ¼ teaspoon of salt and ¼ teaspoon of black pepper evenly.
3. In a shallow bowl, mix together 1 cup of flour, cracker crumbs, baking powder, red chili powder, 1 teaspoon of salt, and ½ teaspoon of black pepper.
4. In another shallow bowl, add eggs and ¾ cup of milk and beat well.
5. Coat steaks with cracker mixture and then dip in milk mixture.
6. Again, coat with cracker mixture evenly.
7. When the temperature indicator light has turned off, fry chicken steaks for about 15 minutes or until golden brown, flipping once after 10 minutes.
8. With a slotted spoon or tongs, transfer chicken steaks onto a paper towel-lined plate to drain.
9. Cover the steaks with foil to keep warm.
10. In a bowl, add remaining 4 cups of milk, ¼ cup of flour, 1 teaspoon of salt, and 1 teaspoon of black pepper and beat until well combined.
11. In a skillet, add 1 tablespoon of oil from fryer with cooking bits over medium-high heat.
12. Add milk mixture, beating continuously until well combined.
13. Cook for about 10-12 minutes, stirring occasionally.
14. Serve chicken steaks alongside gravy with the garnish of parsley.

Preparation time: *15 minutes*
Cooking time: *27 minutes*

CHICKEN FRIED STEAK BITES

These steak bites are a happy alternative to chicken nuggets…and I you'll find them much more enjoyable as well. You may need to go ahead and double the recipe because these tasty morsels will not last. Of course, these are fun to serve for dinner, but they also are great if you are looking for a hearty appetizer.

Ingredients:

For Gravy:

- 2 tablespoons bacon grease
- ¼ cup all-purpose flour
- ¾ teaspoon salt
- ¾ teaspoon coarse ground black pepper
- 3-3½ cups whole milk

For Chicken Steak Bites:

- 2 cups all-purpose flour
- 1½ tablespoons seasoning salt
- 2 teaspoons coarse ground pepper
- 1 egg
- ½ cup milk
- 2 pounds cube steaks, cut into 1½-inch pieces

Preparation time: 15 minutes
Cooking time: 10 minutes

Directions:

1. Prepare fryer and set the temperature to 356 degrees. Cover the fryer with the lid.
2. For gravy: In an 8-inch cast iron skillet, melt bacon grease over medium-high heat.
3. Add flour, salt, and pepper, beating continuously until well combined.
4. Cook until flour becomes golden brown, beating continuously.
5. Slowly add 3 cups of milk, and cook until gravy starts to bubble, beating continuously.
6. Stir in remaining ½ cup of milk if gravy is too thick.
7. Reduce the heat to very low to keep the gravy warm until serving.
8. For chicken steak bites: In a shallow bowl, mix together flour, seasoning salt, and black pepper.
9. In another shallow bowl, add egg and milk and beat until well combined.
10. Coat cube steak pieces with flour and then dip into egg mixture.
11. Again, coat with flour mixture evenly.
12. When the temperature indicator light has turned off, fry cube steak pieces for about 3-4 minutes or until golden brown.
13. With a slotted spoon, transfer steak pieces onto a paper towel-lined plate to drain.
14. Serve chicken fried steak bites alongside gravy.

CORN DOGS

When I was younger, my family used to go to the county fair every summer. They had the best corn dogs ever! Deep fried and crunchy, no frozen food section corn dog could come close. The recipe for these corn dogs takes me back to those summer days. Easy to make and eat, corn dogs are a hit in any family.

Ingredients:

- 1¼ cups all-purpose flour
- 1½ cups yellow cornmeal
- ¼ cup sugar
- 1 tablespoon baking powder
- ¼ teaspoon salt
- 1 egg, beaten
- ½ cup buttermilk
- 1 tablespoon honey
- 1 tablespoon vegetable oil
- 1 (10-count) package hot dogs
- 10 skewers

Preparation time: 15 minutes
Cooking time: 3 minutes

Directions:

1. Prepare fryer and set the temperature to 356 degrees. Cover the fryer with the lid.
2. In a large bowl, mix together flour, cornmeal, sugar, baking powder, and salt.
3. Add egg, buttermilk, honey, and oil and mix until a thick and smooth mixture is formed.
4. With paper towels, pat hot dogs dry.
5. Insert one skewer into each hot dog.
6. Coat hot dogs with batter mixture evenly.
7. When the temperature indicator light has turned off, fry hot dog skewers for about 2-3 minutes or until golden brown.
8. With a slotted spoon, transfer hot dog skewers onto a paper towel-lined plate to drain.
9. Serve immediately.

RIBS

Can barbecue ribs get any better? Um, yeah, by adding them to your T-Fal fryer! Frying ribs creates an amazing crust that is unbelievably tasty. They are packed with flavor the whole way through. I actually like to serve the sauce as a dipping sauce for the side. That way the crust doesn't get too soggy while you're eating.

Ingredients:

For Ribs:

- Rack of baby back ribs, as required (membrane removed)
- Cajun seasoning, to taste
- Flour, for coating

For Sauce:

- 4 ounces BBQ sauce (of your choice)
- 2 tablespoons chipotle adobo
- ¼ cup apple juice

Preparation time: 15 minutes
Cooking time: 12 minutes

Directions:

1. Prepare fryer and set the temperature to 356 degrees. Cover the fryer with the lid.
2. Cut each rib rack into individual ribs.
3. Season ribs with Cajun seasoning and then coat with flour evenly.
4. When the temperature indicator light has turned off, fry ribs for about 12 minutes or until golden brown.
5. For sauce: In a pan, add all ingredients over low heat and cook until thickened.
6. With a slotted spoon, transfer ribs onto a paper towel-lined plate to drain.
7. Coat ribs with sauce or serve with the sauce on the side.

CHEESEBURGER BITES

Our family loves to experiment with different finger foods and the stuffing inside them. We all agreed that these cheeseburger bites have been one of the most successful experiments yet. The nice thing about them is that they can really be tailored to your taste. Try adding bacon bits, Swiss cheese, and mushroom slivers, or even diced jalapeños.

Ingredients:

- 1 pound ground beef
- 1 cup onion, chopped
- 4 tablespoons ketchup
- 2 tablespoons mustard
- 1 cup cheddar cheese, shredded
- 1 package wonton wrappers

Preparation time: *20 minutes*
Cooking time: *13 minutes*

Directions:

1. Heat a nonstick skillet and cook beef and onion for about 8-10 minutes.
2. Remove extra grease from skillet.
3. Stir in ketchup and mustard and remove from heat. Set aside to cool completely.
4. Prepare fryer and set the temperature to 338 degrees. Cover the fryer with the lid.
5. After cooling, add cheese to beef mixture and stir to combine.
6. Spread wrappers out on a smooth surface.
7. Place 1 tablespoon of beef mixture in center of each wonton wrapper. With wet fingers, slightly moisten the edges of each wrapper. Fold the wrapper in a triangle shape and press to seal the filling.
8. Repeat with remaining wrappers and filling mixture.
9. When the temperature indicator light has turned off, fry wrapper for about 2-3 minute or until golden brown on all sides.
10. With a slotted spoon, transfer the wrappers onto a paper towel-lined plate to drain.
11. Serve immediately.

BEEF CHIMICHANGAS

This is my favorite thing to order at a Mexican restaurant. I love the crispy outer shell, smothered in cheese and sour cream, mixed with the warm, spicy meat. I love to create them at home, adding a few extras or all my favorites. It takes a little time, but this is a meal that is well worth it.

Ingredients:

- 1 pound lean ground beef
- ½ cup onion, chopped
- 1 garlic clove, minced
- 1 teaspoon red chili powder
- ½ teaspoon dried oregano, crushed
- ½ teaspoon ground cumin
- 1 (15-ounce) can refried beans
- 1 (15-ounce) can plus 1 (8-ounce) can tomato sauce, divided
- 1 (4½-ounce) can green chilies
- 1 jalapeño pepper, minced
- 8 (10-inch) tortillas, warmed
- 1½ cups Cheddar cheese, shredded
- Sour cream, for topping
- Chopped fresh cilantro, for topping

Directions:

1. Prepare fryer and set the temperature to 374 degrees. Cover the fryer with the lid.
2. Heat a nonstick skillet and cook beef for about 4-5 minutes.
3. Remove extra grease from skillet.
4. Add onion and cook for about 4-5 minutes.
5. Stir in garlic, chili powder, oregano, cumin, and cook for about 1 minute.
6. Stir in refried beans and ½ cup of tomato sauce and remove from heat.
7. For sauce: In a medium pan, add remaining tomato sauce, green chilies, and jalapeño pepper over medium heat and cook until warmed.
8. Arrange tortillas on a smooth surface.
9. Place about 1/3 cup of filling on one side of a tortilla. Fold one side over the filling to cover. Fold in remaining 2 sides and roll up. Secure with toothpicks.
10. Repeat with remaining tortillas.
11. When the temperature indicator light has turned off, fry chimichangas for about 2 minutes per side or until golden brown.
12. With a slotted spoon, transfer chimichangas onto a paper towel-lined plate to drain.
13. Serve chimichangas with the topping of cheese, tomato sauce, sour cream and cilantro.

Preparation time: 20 minutes
Cooking time: 18 minutes

PIZZA

Now you can create a deep-dish pizza right at home by deep frying the dough to create an extra crispy, crunchy crust. Add your favorite toppings and sauce to make it your own special creation.

Ingredients:

- 1 homemade or store-bought pizza dough, about 6-8 inches round
- 3 tablespoons garlic butter
- 1 cup mozzarella cheese, shredded
- ½ onion, sliced
- Pepperoni, as required
- Other desired toppings

Preparation time: 15 minutes
Cooking time: 8 minutes

Directions:

1. Prepare fryer and set the temperature to 374 degrees. Cover the fryer with the lid.
2. Preheat the oven to 350 degrees F. Line a baking sheet with parchment paper. Roll dough into a small 6-8 inch circle, creating a personal pizza
3. When the temperature indicator light has turned off, fry pizza dough for about 2-3 minutes or until golden brown.
4. With a slotted spoon or tongs, transfer pizza dough onto a paper towel-lined plate to drain.
5. Place pizza dough onto prepared baking sheet.
6. Spread garlic butter over dough, followed by mozzarella cheese, sliced onions, pepperoni, and other desired toppings.
7. Bake until cheese is melted completely.
8. Remove from oven and cut into wedges.
9. Serve immediately.

CHILES RELLENOS

Traditional Mexican cuisine always includes chiles rellenos, charred and peeled chile peppers that have been stuffed and fried. In this recipe, I stuff them with cheese and fry 'em up in the T-Fal. Be sure to choose big, firm peppers as this will make the peeling process much easier.

Ingredients:

- 6 fresh Anaheim chile peppers
- 1 (8 ounce) package Queso Asadero cheese, cut into ¾-inch thick strips
- 2 eggs, separated
- 1 teaspoon baking powder
- ¾ cup all-purpose flour

Directions:

1. Preheat the oven to broiler. Place oven rack about 6 inches from heating element. Line a baking sheet with a piece of foil.
2. Arrange chile peppers onto prepared baking sheet in a single layer.
3. Broil for about 10 minutes, flipping occasionally.
4. Prepare fryer and set the temperature to 356 degrees. Cover the fryer with the lid.
5. Remove peppers from oven and transfer blackened peppers to a bowl.
6. Cover the bowl tightly with plastic wrap and set aside for about 15 minutes.
7. Once cool, rinse peppers under cold water to peel off skins.
8. Carefully cut a slit along the long side of each pepper to remove seeds and core.
9. Rinse the peppers inside and out and with paper towels pat dry completely.
10. Stuff the peppers with cheese strips.
11. In a shallow bowl, place flour.
12. In another shallow bowl, add egg yolks and baking powder and beat until well combined.
13. In a small metal bowl, add egg whites and beat until stiff peaks form with an electric mixer.
14. Slowly fold beaten egg whites into yolk mixture.
15. Coat stuffed pepper with flour, tap off excess flour.
16. Then, dip peppers into egg mixture evenly.
17. When the temperature indicator light has turned off, fry peppers for about 5 minutes per side or until golden brown.
18. With a slotted spoon, transfer peppers onto a paper towel-lined plate to drain.
19. Serve immediately.

Preparation time: 20 minutes
Cooking time: 20 minutes

LASAGNA FRITTA

Be prepared to make the ultimate comfort food using lasagna noodles, layering with cheese and deep frying to golden perfection. Serve with marinara or Alfredo sauce, whichever is your favorite.

Ingredients:

- 10 lasagna noodles
- 1 (15-ounce) container ricotta cheese
- 1 cup mozzarella cheese, shredded
- 4 eggs, divided and beaten
- 2 garlic cloves, minced
- 1 teaspoon Italian seasoning
- Salt and ground black pepper, to taste
- ½ cup all-purpose flour
- 2 cups Italian breadcrumbs
- ¼ cup fresh parsley, finely chopped

Preparation time: 20 minutes
Cooking time: 16 minutes

Directions:

1. In a pot of salted boiling water, prepare lasagna noodles according to package's directions for al dente.
2. Drain noodles well and spread out flat on a greased baking sheet.
3. In a large bowl, add ricotta cheese, mozzarella cheese, 1 egg, garlic, Italian seasoning, salt, and black pepper and mix until well combined.
4. Spread cheese mixture over noodles evenly.
5. Fold each noodle 3-4 times until a square is formed.
6. Freeze for about 30-45 minutes.
7. Prepare fryer and set the temperature to 338 degrees. Cover the fryer with the lid.
8. In 3 shallow bowls, place flour, remaining 3 beaten eggs, and breadcrumbs respectively.
9. Coat noodle squares with flour, dip into eggs, and then coat with breadcrumbs.
10. When the temperature indicator light has turned off, fry noodle squares for about 2-3 minutes per side or until golden brown.
11. With a slotted spoon, transfer noodle squares onto a paper towel-lined plate to drain.
12. Serve immediately with the garnish of parsley.

RAVIOLI

A delicious meal or snack, fried ravioli couldn't be easier to prepare. I like to use both parmesan cheese as well as breadcrumbs and seasoning for the outer coating for additional flavor. Serve with marinara sauce for dipping.

Ingredients:

- 2 eggs
- 1 cup breadcrumbs
- ½ cup parmesan cheese, finely shredded
- 1 teaspoon dried parsley, crushed
- ½ teaspoon oregano, crushed
- ¼ teaspoon dried basil, crushed
- ½ teaspoon garlic salt
- 8-10 ounces fresh ravioli

Preparation time: 15 minutes
Cooking time: 3 minutes

Directions:

1. Prepare fryer and set the temperature to 374 degrees. Cover the fryer with the lid.
2. In a shallow bowl, beat eggs.
3. In another shallow bowl, mix together remaining ingredients except ravioli.
4. With paper towels, pat ravioli dry.
5. Dip ravioli in egg and then coat with breadcrumb mixture evenly.
6. When the temperature indicator light has turned off, fry ravioli for about 3 minutes or until golden brown, flipping once halfway.
7. With a slotted spoon, transfer ravioli onto a paper towel-lined plate to drain.
8. Serve immediately.

EGGPLANT PARMESAN

There is a restaurant in Atlanta that claims to have labor-inducing eggplant parmesan. Apparently, over 300 babies have been born within a few days of their mothers eating the restaurant's eggplant parm. I can't make that kind of claim with this recipe, but I think you'll love it anyway. Using the T-Fal to deep fry your eggplant ensures that it will be perfectly golden brown and crisp.

Ingredients:

- 1 large eggplant, cut into ½-inch thick slices
- 2 tablespoons kosher salt
- ½ cup milk
- 3 eggs
- 1½ cups Italian seasoned breadcrumbs
- 3 cups marinara sauce
- 2 cups whole milk mozzarella cheese, shredded
- 1 cup parmesan cheese, shredded
- Chopped fresh basil leaves, for garnishing

Directions:

1. Sprinkle eggplant slices with salt evenly and place in a large colander for about 45-60 minutes.
2. Brush off all excess salt from eggplant slices.
3. Prepare fryer and set the temperature to 356 degrees. Cover the fryer with the lid.
4. Preheat the oven to 375 degrees F.
5. In a shallow bowl, add milk and eggs and beat well.
6. In another shallow bowl, place breadcrumbs.
7. Dip eggplant slices into egg mixture evenly and then coat with breadcrumbs, shaking off the excess.
8. When the temperature indicator light has turned off, fry eggplant slices for about 2-3 minutes per side or until golden brown.
9. With a slotted spoon, transfer eggplant slices onto a paper towel-lined plate to drain.
10. In the bottom of a large casserole dish, pour in marinara sauce in an even layer and top with a layer of fried eggplant slices.
11. Place ¼ cup of marinara sauce on top of the eggplant slices and sprinkle with a generous amount of mozzarella cheese.
12. Repeat the layers and finally, top with parmesan cheese.
13. Bake for about 20-25 minutes or until the cheese is bubbly and top becomes golden brown.
14. Serve hot with a sprinkle of basil.

Preparation time: 20 minutes
Cooking time: 31 minutes

RICOTTA & SAGE MEATBALLS

These are quite unique and worthy of serving at your most special occasions. They do take a little time to prepare, but they are probably not something many of your guests will have ever had. I love the crisp shell that forms around the savory meatballs. Serve with marinara sauce and freshly grated parmesan cheese.

Ingredients:

- 1/3 cup whole-milk ricotta
- 2 tablespoons vegetable oil
- 3 garlic cloves, minced
- 2 teaspoons fennel seeds, toasted and lightly crushed
- 1¼ teaspoons dried sage, crushed
- 1 teaspoon red pepper flakes, crushed
- 1 teaspoon kosher salt
- ½ teaspoon freshly ground black pepper
- 8 ounces ground pork
- 24 fresh sage leaves
- ¾ cup all-purpose flour
- 1 large egg, beaten
- 2 cups panko breadcrumbs
- Marinara sauce, warmed

Preparation time: *20 minutes*
Cooking time: *16 minutes*

Directions:

1. Prepare fryer and set the temperature to 356 degrees. Cover the fryer with the lid.
2. Preheat the oven to 275 degrees Fahrenheit.
3. Line a baking sheet with parchment and place a wire rack on top.
4. In a bowl, add ricotta and oil and mix until smooth.
5. Add garlic, fennel seeds, sage, red pepper flakes, salt, and black pepper and mix until well combined.
6. Add pork and mix until just combined.
7. With damp hands, make about 1-inch balls from mixture.
8. Wrap 1 sage leaf around each ball, pressing gently to adhere.
9. In 3 different shallow bowls, place flour, beaten egg, and breadcrumbs respectively.
10. Coat meatballs with flour, dip in egg and then coat with breadcrumbs evenly.
11. When the temperature indicator light has turned off, fry meatballs for about 1 minute or until golden brown.
12. With a slotted spoon, transfer meatballs onto a paper towel-lined plate to drain.
13. Now, place meatballs onto prepared baking sheet on top of the wire rack.
14. Bake in the pre-heated oven for about 15 minutes.
15. Serve with a topping of marinara sauce.

ITALIAN ARANCINI RICE BALLS

These are basically fried risotto balls, and if you haven't ever given them a try, you are in for a treat. When you bite into them, the crisp outer coating gives way to creamy, cheesy rice, the best of both worlds. It is helpful if you can prepare the rice the day before to help it stick together and form a ball.

Ingredients:

For Rice Balls:

- 2 tablespoons butter
- 1 small onion, finely chopped
- 2 garlic cloves, minced
- 1½ cups Arborio rice
- ½ cup white wine
- 3½ cups chicken broth
- 1 cup milk
- 1 cup cheddar cheese, grated
- ¾ cup mozzarella cheese, grated
- 1 egg
- 2½ tablespoons fresh parsley, finely chopped
- ½ teaspoon salt
- Freshly ground black pepper, to taste

For Coating

- ½ cup all-purpose flour
- ½ teaspoon salt
- Freshly ground black pepper, to taste
- 2 eggs
- 2 cups panko breadcrumbs

Directions:

1. Preheat the oven to 350 degrees F.
2. For rice balls: In an ovenproof skillet, melt butter over medium heat and sauté onion and garlic for about 5 minutes.
3. Add rice and sauté until translucent.
4. Stir in wine and increase heat to medium-high. Cook until liquid is mostly absorbed.
5. Stir in chicken broth and milk and bring to simmer.
6. Cover the skillet and transfer into oven. Bake, covered, for about 30-40 minutes or until all liquid is absorbed.
7. Remove from oven and set aside to cool.
8. After cooling, add remaining ingredients and mix until well combined.
9. Refrigerate, covered, for at least 3 hours or overnight.
10. Prepare fryer and set the temperature to 374 degrees. Cover the fryer with the lid.
11. In a shallow bowl, mix together flour, salt, and black pepper.
12. In a second shallow bowl, beat eggs lightly.
13. In a third shallow bowl, place breadcrumbs.
14. Scoop out about 2½ tablespoon of mixture and form into a ball. Repeat with remaining rice.
15. Coat rice balls with flour mixture and then dip in eggs and finally, coat with breadcrumbs evenly.
16. When the temperature indicator light has turned off, fry rice balls for about 2-3 minutes or until golden brown.
17. With a slotted spoon, transfer rice balls onto a paper towel-lined plate to drain.
18. Serve immediately.

Preparation time: *20 minutes*
Cooking time: *55 minutes*

MONTE CRISTO

Is it dessert, or is it lunch? It's hard to tell with this sandwich, but either way I will call it delicious. Crisp on the outside with melty cheese in the middle, you have to try this baby. Serve with a side of jelly for dipping and a sprinkle of powdered sugar.

Ingredients:

For Sandwiches:

- 3 whole wheat sandwich bread slices
- 1 cheddar cheese slice (deli-style)
- 3 ounces sliced ham (deli-style)
- 1 Swiss cheese slice(deli-style)
- 3 ounces sliced turkey (deli-style)

For Coating:

- 1 cup all-purpose flour
- 2 egg yolks
- 1 cup ice water
- 1 teaspoon baking soda

For serving:

- Powdered sugar, as required
- Raspberry preserves, as required

Preparation time: 15 minutes
Cooking time: 6 minutes

Directions:

1. Prepare fryer and set the temperature to 374 degrees. Cover the fryer with the lid.
2. Arrange a bread slice on a plate and top with cheddar slice, followed by ham, second bread slice, turkey, Swiss cheese, and third bread slice.
3. With the palm of your hand, press the sandwich to flatten it a little.
4. Cut the sandwich in half diagonally and insert toothpick into each corner.
5. For coating: In a shallow dish, add all ingredients and mix until smooth.
6. Dip sandwich halves into egg mixture evenly.
7. When the temperature indicator light has turned off, fry sandwich halves for about 2-3 minutes per side or until golden brown.
8. With tongs, transfer sandwich halves onto a paper towel-lined plate to drain.
9. Now, cut each sandwich half in half to make 4 pieces.
10. Dust sandwiches with powdered sugar and serve with raspberry preserves.

GRILLED CHEESE

This grilled cheese recipe is incredible. It takes common ordinary comfort food that we all love and makes it even better. You can certainly adapt the recipe to make your favorite grilled cheese sandwich by changing the bread or the type of cheese used. You can even add little slivers of tomato, avocado, or even bacon.

Ingredients:

- ½ cup mayonnaise
- 8 hearty white bread slices
- 8 white American cheese slices
- 2/3 cup milk
- 2 large eggs
- 1½ sleeves Ritz crackers, crushed into coarse crumbs

Preparation time: *15 minutes*
Cooking time: *4 minutes*

Directions:

1. Spread mayonnaise over each bread slice evenly.
2. Arrange cheese slices over 4 bread slices and cover with remaining bread slices, mayonnaise side down.
3. Carefully cut each sandwich in quarters.
4. In a shallow dish, add milk and eggs and beat well.
5. In another shallow dish place cracker crumbs.
6. Dip each quarter in the egg and then coat with crackers.
7. Arrange sandwiches onto a parchment-lined baking sheet and refrigerate for about 1 hour.
8. Prepare fryer and set the temperature to 320 degrees. Cover the fryer with the lid.
9. When the temperature indicator light has turned off, fry sandwiches for about 1-2 minutes per side or until golden brown.
10. With a slotted spoon, transfer sandwiches onto a paper towel-lined plate to drain.

PEANUT BUTTER & JELLY SANDWICH

While eating at a restaurant on vacation, one of our kids ordered a peanut butter and jelly sandwich for lunch. Imagine our surprise (and excitement) when she was served a fried peanut butter and jelly. Fortunately for my wife and I, she wasn't a big fan, but we sure enjoyed it! The peanut butter and jelly seem to melt in the middle, surrounded by a crunchy outer shell. Don't skip out on trying this decadent sandwich. My daughter still won't eat these, but trust me. They're killer.

Ingredients:

- 4 slices white bread, crusts removed
- 6-8 tablespoons peanut butter
- 4-6 tablespoons jelly (strawberry or grape)
- 1 cup all-purpose flour
- ¼ cup granulated sugar
- 1 teaspoon baking powder
- 1 teaspoon kosher salt
- ½-¾ cup milk
- 2 eggs, beaten
- 1 teaspoon vanilla extract
- Powdered sugar, for dusting

Preparation time: 10 minutes
Cooking time: 5 minutes

Directions:

1. Prepare fryer and set the temperature to 320 degrees. Cover the fryer with the lid.
2. Remove crusts from bread and spread peanut butter onto two of the slices. Spread jelly on remaining two slices.
3. Press peanut butter and jelly slices together forming two sandwiches.
4. In a bowl, mix together flour, sugar, baking powder, and salt.
5. Add ½ cup of milk, beaten eggs, and vanilla and beat until smooth. More milk may be added if batter seems too thick.
6. Dip each sandwich in batter evenly and let the excess mixture drip back into the bowl.
7. When the temperature indicator light has turned off, fry sandwiches for about 2-2½ minutes per side or until golden brown.
8. With tongs, transfer sandwiches onto a paper towel-lined plate to drain.
9. Serve warm sandwiches with a sprinkle of powdered sugar.

Side Dishes

MAC 'N CHEESE BALLS

If you are looking for a fun, clever way to serve a traditional side dish, look no further than this recipe for fried mac 'n cheese balls. You and your friends or family will love the crispy coating surrounding the warm cheesy noodles. Plus, it's just so much fun to eat food that is bite-sized.

Ingredients:

- 2 cups prepared macaroni and cheese, chilled overnight
- ¾ cup flour
- 2 eggs, beaten
- 2 cups panko breadcrumbs

Preparation time: 15 minutes
Cooking time: 2 minutes

Directions:

1. Prepare fryer and set the temperature to 356 degrees. Cover the fryer with the lid.
2. With your hands, form the macaroni and cheese into 1½-inch balls.
3. In 3 different shallow bowls, place flour, eggs, and breadcrumbs respectively.
4. Coat balls with flour, dip into eggs, and finally coat with breadcrumbs.
5. When the temperature indicator light has turned off, fry balls for about 1 minute per side or until golden brown.
6. With a slotted spoon, transfer balls onto a paper towel-lined plate to drain.
7. Serve immediately.

HUSH PUPPIES

Hush puppies are savory, golden fried balls of cornmeal and they are wonderful served with fish. The name hush puppy is often attributed to Confederate soldiers who would fry up little scraps of cornmeal and toss them to their dogs to quiet them in the Civil War. Most modern day fish fries would not be complete without a big portion of hush puppies.

Ingredients:

- 2 tablespoons butter
- 1 medium onion, chopped
- 1½ cups self-rising cornmeal
- ¾ cup all-purpose flour
- 2 tablespoons sugar
- 1 teaspoon baking powder
- ½ teaspoon baking soda
- ½ teaspoon salt
- 1¼ cups buttermilk
- 1 large egg, beaten

Preparation time: 15 minutes
Cooking time: 15 minutes

Directions:

1. In a skillet, melt butter and cook onion until caramelized.
2. Remove from heat and set aside to cool.
3. Prepare fryer and set the temperature to 356 degrees. Cover the fryer with the lid.
4. In a bowl, mix together cornmeal, flour, sugar, baking powder, baking soda, and salt.
5. Add buttermilk and egg and beat until just combined.
6. Fold in cooked onions and set aside for about 10 minutes.
7. When the temperature indicator light has turned off, drop tablespoons of mixture into the oil and fry for about 2-3 minutes or until golden brown.
8. With a slotted spoon, transfer hush puppies onto a paper towel-lined plate to drain.
9. Serve immediately.

LOADED MASHED POTATO BITES

If you're into potato skins, you'll love these mashed potato bites. They still have a little crunch like a potato skin, while being creamy, soft, and cheesy in the center. Serve them by themselves or with a side of sour cream.

Ingredients:

- 3 cups prepared mashed potatoes, room temperature
- 1½ cups sharp cheddar cheese, shredded
- ¾ cup cooked bacon, crumbled
- ½ cup scallions, chopped
- 1 cup Colby Jack cheese cubes, ½-inch cubes
- 1 egg, beaten
- ½ cup parmesan cheese, grated
- ½ cup panko breadcrumbs
- Salt and freshly ground black pepper, to taste

Preparation time: *15 minutes*
Cooking time: *3 minutes*

Directions:

1. In a large bowl, add potatoes, cheddar cheese, bacon, and onions and mix until well combined.
2. With an ice cream scoop, make 1-inch balls of the potato mixture.
3. Push 1 Colby Jack cube into the center of each ball and then roll the ball again.
4. Arrange the balls onto a plate and refrigerate for about 30 minutes.
5. Prepare fryer and set the temperature to 374 degrees. Cover the fryer with the lid.
6. In a shallow bowl, place the egg.
7. In another shallow bowl, mix together parmesan, breadcrumbs, salt, and pepper.
8. Dip each potato ball into egg, shake off the excess, and then coat with breadcrumb mixture.
9. When the temperature indicator light has turned off, fry potato ball for about 2-3 minutes or until golden brown.
10. With a slotted spoon, transfer potato ball onto a paper towel-lined plate to drain.
11. Serve immediately.

ZUCCHINI ROUNDS

Whenever I have an abundance of zucchini in the garden (which is every summer) I enjoy making these fried zucchini. Cut them thick enough that they will hold up in the fryer and you can still taste the zucchini. I like to eat them with ranch dressing, but you may prefer marinara sauce.

Ingredients:

- 2 cups all-purpose flour
- 2-3 large eggs
- 1 tablespoon fresh parsley, chopped
- Coarse salt, to taste
- 3 cups Italian seasoned breadcrumbs
- 1 cup parmesan cheese, grated
- 2 pounds medium zucchini, sliced into ¼-½-inch-thick rounds
- Marinara sauce, for dipping

Preparation time: 15 minutes
Cooking time: 3 minutes

Directions:

1. Prepare fryer and set the temperature to 356 degrees. Cover the fryer with the lid.
2. In a shallow bowl, place flour.
3. In a second shallow bowl, add eggs, parsley and a pinch of salt and beat until well combined.
4. In a third shallow bowl, mix together breadcrumbs and cheese.
5. Coat zucchini rounds with flour and then dip in egg mixture allowing excess to drip off and finally, coat with breadcrumbs mixture evenly.
6. When the temperature indicator light has turned off, fry zucchini rounds for about 2-3 minutes or until golden brown.
7. With a slotted spoon, transfer zucchini rounds onto a paper towel-lined plate to drain.
8. Sprinkle with some salt and serve immediately alongside marinara sauce.

CAULIFLOWER

Cauliflower ain't just for vegetarians. Sure, they're loaded with vitamins C and K and said to fight cancer and stimulate heart and brain health. And while it may not be exactly "healthy" when it's deep fried…you're still getting your vegetables. It also tastes amazing.

Ingredients:

- 1 cup flour
- ½ cup cornstarch
- 1 teaspoon baking powder
- ½ teaspoon salt
- 1 cup water
- 1 tablespoon hot sauce
- 2 cups Italian seasoned breadcrumbs
- 1 small head cauliflower, cut into small pieces

Preparation time: 15 minutes
Cooking time: 6 minutes

Directions:

1. Prepare fryer and set the temperature to 356 degrees. Cover the fryer with the lid.
2. In a large shallow bowl, mix together flour, cornstarch, baking powder, and salt.
3. Add water and hot sauce and mix until a smooth mixture is formed.
4. In another shallow bowl, place breadcrumbs.
5. Dip cauliflower pieces in wet mixture and then coat with breadcrumbs evenly.
6. When the temperature indicator light has turned off, fry cauliflower pieces for about 4-6 minutes or until golden brown.
7. With a slotted spoon, transfer cauliflower pieces onto a paper towel-lined plate to drain.
8. Sprinkle with some salt and serve immediately.

GREEN TOMATOES

I'm crazy about fried green tomatoes and I have yet to order them in a restaurant where they taste better than mine that I prepare at home in my T-Fal. This recipe is simple and delicious. Green tomatoes have a bit of a tart flavor and they really don't need much extra seasoning. The key is to cut them thick enough that they hold together, but you still have plenty of crispy breading in each bite. Serve with ranch dressing or your favorite sauce for dipping.

Ingredients:

- 3 large, green tomatoes, cored and cut into ½-inch thick slices
- Salt, to taste
- ½ cup flour
- 2 eggs, beaten
- 1 cup unseasoned panko breadcrumbs
- ¾ teaspoon onion powder
- ¾ teaspoon garlic powder
- ¼ teaspoon cayenne pepper
- Freshly ground black pepper, to taste

Preparation time: 15 minutes
Cooking time: 5 minutes

Directions:

1. Sprinkle tomato slices lightly with salt and set aside in a colander for at least 20 minutes.
2. Prepare fryer and set the temperature to 356 degrees. Cover the fryer with the lid.
3. In a shallow bowl, place flour.
4. In a second shallow bowl, place beaten eggs.
5. In a third shallow bowl, mix together remaining ingredients and some salt.
6. Coat tomato slices with flour, dip in eggs, and finally, coat with breadcrumb mixture, shaking off excess.
7. When the temperature indicator light has turned off, fry tomato slices for about 2-3 minutes. Flip over and fry for about 1-2 minutes or until golden brown.
8. With a slotted spoon, transfer tomato slices onto a paper towel-lined plate to drain.
9. Serve immediately.

CRISPY & CHEESY BROCCOLI

What a great way to get kids and picky adults to eat their broccoli. The double coating of a flour mixture and a liquid batter helps to achieve a crisp, golden fry. I like to use sharp cheddar cheese, as it complements the broccoli so well, but use whatever you have on hand.

Ingredients:

- ¾ cup all-purpose flour, divided
- 4 tablespoons cheddar cheese, finely shredded and divided
- ¼ teaspoon onion powder
- 1 cup buttermilk
- ½ teaspoon baking powder
- ¼ teaspoon salt
- ¼ teaspoon black pepper
- 3 cups broccoli florets, patted dry

Preparation time: 15 minutes
Cooking time: 2 minutes

Directions:

1. Prepare fryer and set the temperature to 356 degrees. Cover the fryer with the lid.
2. In a shallow bowl, mix together ¼ cup of flour, 2 tablespoons of cheese, and onion powder.
3. Ina second shallow bowl, add remaining ½ cup of flour, 2 tablespoons of cheese, buttermilk, baking powder, salt, and black pepper and mix until smooth.
4. Coat broccoli florets with flour mixture and then dip into buttermilk mixture evenly.
5. When the temperature indicator light has turned off, fry broccoli florets for about 1-2 minutes or until golden brown.
6. With a slotted spoon, transfer broccoli florets onto a paper towel-lined plate to drain.
7. Serve immediately.

CORN

Corn on the cob is always a delicious summer treat and it's even better with a light crunchy coating. I had seen this served at a state fair and although it doesn't change the wonderful flavor of the corn, it adds a little novelty and flavorful crisp coating. And let's not kids ourselves, EVERYTHING is better when it's fried!

Ingredients:

- 1 egg, beaten
- 1 cup milk
- 1½ cups flour
- 1 teaspoon seasoning salt
- ½ teaspoon ground black pepper
- 6 ears corn, husks and silk removed

Preparation time: 15 minutes
Cooking time: 5 minutes

Directions:

1. Prepare fryer and set the temperature to 338 degrees. Cover the fryer with the lid.
2. In a shallow bowl, add egg and milk and beat well.
3. In another shallow bowl, mix together flour, seasoning salt, and black pepper.
4. Dip each ear of corn into milk mixture and then coat with flour mixture, shaking off excess flour.
5. When the temperature indicator light has turned off, fry ear of corn for about 5 minutes or until golden brown.
6. With a slotted spoon, transfer ear of corn onto a paper towel-lined plate to drain.
7. Serve immediately.

OKRA

Fired okra is a staple of Southern livin'. I don't know that I have ever had okra that hasn't been breaded and fried. You can adjust the seasoning to make it spicier by adding more hot sauce or cayenne pepper as many people like their okra with a bit of kick to it.

Ingredients:

- 1¼ pounds fresh okra, sliced and ends removed
- 1 cup plus 2 tablespoons all-purpose flour, divided
- Salt and freshly ground black pepper, to taste
- 1 cup whole buttermilk
- 1 teaspoon hot sauce
- ½ cup yellow self-rising cornmeal
- ½ teaspoon paprika
- ¼-½ teaspoon cayenne pepper
- ½ teaspoon onion powder
- ¼ teaspoon garlic powder
- 1 teaspoon salt
- ¼ teaspoon freshly ground black pepper

Preparation time: *15 minutes*
Cooking time: *4 minutes*

Directions:

1. Prepare fryer and set the temperature to 338 degrees. Cover the fryer with the lid.
2. Dust okra slices with 2 tablespoons of flour and sprinkle lightly with salt and black pepper.
3. In a shallow bowl, mix together buttermilk and hot sauce.
4. In another shallow bowl, sift together remaining 1 cup of flour, cornmeal, spices, salt, and black pepper.
5. Dip okra slices in buttermilk mixture and then coat with cornmeal mixture, shaking off any excess.
6. When the temperature indicator light has turned off, fry okra slices for about 4 minutes or until golden brown.
7. With a slotted spoon, transfer okra slices onto a paper towel-lined plate to drain.
8. Serve immediately.

ARTICHOKE HEARTS

This recipe is quite simple as you can just use canned artichoke hearts that are pretty much ready to go. Adjust the cheesiness of the coating by adding more or less parmesan cheese, according to your taste. This is wonderful served with a lemon garlic dipping sauce.

Ingredients:

- ½ cup milk
- 2 eggs
- 1½ cups seasoned dry breadcrumbs
- ¼ cup parmesan cheese, grated
- 1 (15-ounce) can artichoke hearts, drained and quartered

Preparation time: 15 minutes
Cooking time: 3 minutes

Directions:

1. Prepare fryer and set the temperature to 374 degrees. Cover the fryer with the lid.
2. In a shallow bowl, add milk and eggs and beat well.
3. In another shallow bowl, place breadcrumbs and parmesan cheese. Mix briefly.
4. Dip artichoke hearts in egg mixture and then coat evenly with breadcrumbs.
5. When the temperature indicator light has turned off, fry artichokes for about 2-3 minutes or until golden brown.
6. With a slotted spoon, transfer onto a paper towel-lined plate to drain.
7. Serve immediately.

SPICY BRUSSELS SPROUTS

This is such a simple recipe that delivers fantastic results. It is a wonderful side dish, especially if you like things a little spicy. Tossing the Brussels sprouts in the fryer cooks them and makes them slightly crisp around the edges. Toss them in a sauce that takes two minutes to stir together and you have a delicious new take on this vegetable.

Ingredients:

- 1½ pounds Brussels sprouts, quartered
- 2 ounces mayonnaise
- ¼ ounce Sriracha sauce
- 1 teaspoon fresh lime juice

Preparation time: 15 minutes
Cooking time: 5 minutes

Directions:

1. Prepare fryer and set the temperature to 374 degrees. Cover the fryer with the lid.
2. When the temperature indicator light has turned off, fry Brussels sprouts for about 5 minutes or until golden brown.
3. With a slotted spoon, transfer Brussels sprouts onto a paper towel-lined plate to drain.
4. Meanwhile in a bowl, add remaining ingredients and mix well.
5. Add Brussels sprouts and toss to coat well.
6. Serve immediately.

VIDALIA ONION RINGS

Even though I'm not a huge fan of onions, I do love a good onion ring. Vidalia onions are grown in Georgia and are considerably sweeter than most other varieties of onions, making them the perfect candidate to batter and fry. Double-coating the onions in the flour mixture gives them a thick, crisp coating. Serve with your favorite dipping sauce.

Ingredients:

- 2 Vidalia onions, cut into ½-inch thick rings
- 2 cups flour
- 2 teaspoons paprika
- 2 teaspoons garlic powder
- 2 teaspoons salt
- 1 teaspoon ground black pepper
- 1 cup milk
- 2 eggs

Preparation time: 15 minutes
Cooking time: 3 minutes

Directions:

1. Prepare fryer and set the temperature to 356 degrees. Cover the fryer with the lid.
2. Gently separate the rings of onions.
3. In a shallow bowl, mix together flour, paprika, garlic powder, salt, and black pepper.
4. In another shallow bowl, add milk and eggs and beat well.
5. Coat onion rings with flour mixture, dip into egg mixture and finally, coat with flour mixture again.
6. When the temperature indicator light has turned off, fry onion rings for about 1½ minutes per side or until golden brown.
7. With a slotted spoon, transfer onion rings onto a paper towel-lined plate to drain.
8. Sprinkle with salt and serve immediately.

CRISPY FRENCH FRIES

These crispy French fries have an extra coating that adds a satisfying crunch that regular French fries just don't have. Cut the strips of potatoes fairly thin, about half an inch by a quarter inch. This way they will cook evenly and become a delicious golden brown. Serve with ketchup or dipping sauce of your choice.

Ingredients:

- 1 cup self-rising flour
- 1 teaspoon Cajun seasoning
- ½ teaspoon salt
- ½ teaspoon ground black pepper
- 4 large Russet potatoes, peeled and cut into strips lengthwise

Preparation time: 15 minutes
Cooking time: 3 minutes

Directions:

1. Prepare fryer and set the temperature to 356 degrees. Cover the fryer with the lid.
2. In a large bowl, mix together all ingredients except potatoes.
3. Add potatoes and toss to coat well.
4. When the temperature indicator light has turned off, fry potatoes for about 5 minutes or until golden brown, flipping once after 2 minutes.
5. With a slotted spoon, transfer the potato fries onto a paper towel-lined plate to drain.
6. Serve immediately.

HOMEMADE POTATO CHIPS

If you love eating kettle-cooked potato chips from a bag, then you will LOVE eating these homemade chips you prepare in your T-Fal. Use a mandolin to cut the potatoes so all the chips will be super thin and have a uniform thickness. Be careful with those mandolins though. To achieve crisp chips, you must soak the potato slices according to the directions.

Ingredients:

- 4 medium potatoes, peeled and sliced paper-thin
- 3 tablespoons salt

Preparation time: 15 minutes
Cooking time: 5 minutes

Directions:

1. In a large bowl of water, dip potato slices and drain well.
2. Now, in the same bowl, add water and salt.
3. Soak potato slices for at least 30 minutes.
4. Drain, then rinse with plain water and again, drain completely.
5. Prepare fryer and set the temperature to 374 degrees. Cover the fryer with the lid.
6. When the temperature indicator light has turned off, fry potato chips for about 5 minutes or until golden brown.
7. With a slotted spoon, transfer potato chips onto a paper towel-lined plate to drain.
8. Serve immediately.

SWEET POTATO FRIES

Sweet potatoes are loaded with fiber and vitamins A and C. They taste great lightly sprinkled with a sugar and spice mixture. The mixture of cornstarch and club soda helps to keep the potatoes crisp in the fryer. No soggy sweet potato fries for you!

Ingredients:

- 1 cup cornstarch
- ¾ cup club soda, cold
- 2 pounds sweet potatoes, peeled and cut into ½-¼-inch fries
- 1/8 teaspoon sugar
- ½ teaspoon garlic powder
- ½ teaspoon smoked paprika
- 1 teaspoon kosher salt

Preparation time: 15 minutes
Cooking time: 8 minutes

Directions:

1. Prepare fryer and set the temperature to 374 degrees. Cover the fryer with the lid.
2. In a shallow bowl, add cornstarch and club soda and beat until well combined.
3. Dip sweet potato fries in soda mixture evenly and let any excess to drip off.
4. When the temperature indicator light has turned off, fry sweet potato fries for about 6-8 minutes or until golden brown.
5. With a slotted spoon, transfer sweet potato fries onto a paper towel-lined plate to drain.
6. Meanwhile in a small bowl, mix together remaining ingredients.
7. Sprinkle fries with sugar and spice mixture and serve.

TATER TOTS

My family loves these crispy, crunchy tater tots. It does take a while to grate the potatoes, but there is just nothing like homemade tots. Be sure to remove as much moisture as possible from the potatoes so they will stick together and fry up crispy.

Ingredients:

- 2 pounds russet potatoes, peeled
- 1 tablespoon all-purpose flour
- 1 teaspoon garlic powder
- ½ teaspoon onion powder
- ¼ teaspoon dried dill, crushed
- ¼ teaspoon dried oregano, crushed
- Kosher salt and freshly ground black pepper, to taste
- 2 tablespoons fresh parsley leaves, chopped

Preparation time: 15 minutes
Cooking time: 4 minutes

Directions:

1. In a large pot of boiling water, cook potatoes for about 6-7 minutes.
2. Drain well and set aside to cool.
3. Prepare fryer and set the temperature to 374 degrees. Cover the fryer with the lid.
4. With a box grater, finely shred potatoes.
5. With a clean dish towel, squeeze potatoes completely, removing moisture.
6. In a large bowl, add potatoes and remaining ingredients except parsley and mix until well combined.
7. Shape potatoes into tots.
8. When the temperature indicator light has turned off, fry tater tots for about 3-4 minutes or until golden brown.
9. With a slotted spoon, transfer tater tots onto a paper towel-lined plate to drain.
10. Serve immediately with a garnish of parsley.

AVOCADO FRIES

Of course, there is nothing wrong with regular French fries, but I love avocados, too. Avocados are creamy and have such wonderful flavor. These fries are crispy on the outside and almost buttery on the inside. Serve with a chipotle mayonnaise dipping sauce.

Ingredients:

- 2 ripe avocados, peeled, halved, and pitted
- Breadcrumbs, as required
- 2 eggs
- Salt, to taste

Preparation time: 15 minutes
Cooking time: 5 minutes

Directions:

1. Prepare fryer and set the temperature to 338 degrees. Cover the fryer with the lid.
2. With a large spoon, fully scoop the avocado flesh. (Make sure to keep avocado flesh intact).
3. Place avocado flesh onto a cutting board, flat side down and with a kitchen knife, cut into ¾-inch wide strips lengthwise
4. In a shallow bowl, place breadcrumbs.
5. In another shallow bowl, beat eggs.
6. Coat avocado strips with breadcrumbs and then dip into eggs.
7. When the temperature indicator light has turned off, fry avocado strips for about 3-5 minutes or until golden brown.
8. With a slotted spoon, transfer avocado strips onto a paper towel-lined plate to drain.
9. Serve immediately.

FRIED EGGPLANT

In the summer, eggplant is a staple at many farmers markets. If you have some readily available, you won't want to miss the opportunity to fry it up at home. Eggplant has a wonderful, rich flavor and tastes so good when fried to a crisp, golden brown. Serve with marinara or a spicy mayonnaise for dipping.

Ingredients:

- 6 eggs
- 1 tablespoon water
- 3-4 cups Italian breadcrumbs
- 1 large fresh eggplant, peeled and cut into 1/2 inch slices
- 2 tsp salt

Directions:

1. Place the eggplant slices on a paper towel or in a collander. Sprinkle each slice lightly with the salt and allow to sit for about 30 minutes.
2. Rinse the eggplant to remove the salt and pat dry with paper towels.
3. Prepare fryer and set the temperature to 356 degrees. Cover the fryer with the lid.
4. In a shallow bowl, add eggs and water and beat well.
5. In another shallow bowl, place breadcrumbs.
6. Dip eggplant slices in egg mixture, letting excess drip off and then coat with breadcrumbs.
7. When the temperature indicator light has turned off, fry eggplant slices for about 3-4 minutes. Flip the side and cook for about 2-3 minutes or until golden brown.
8. With a slotted spoon, transfer eggplant slices onto a paper towel-lined plate to drain.
9. Serve immediately.

Preparation time: 15 minutes
Cooking time: 7 minutes

JALAPEÑO CORN FRITTERS

Corn fritters are always great, but I think these jalapeño corn fritters are even more amazing. Some bites pack a wonderfully spicy punch and every bite is filled with savory corn and cheese. These are particularly good served with a side of spicy mayo for dipping.

Ingredients:

- ¼ cup all-purpose flour
- 2 large eggs, beaten
- 2 tablespoons parmesan cheese, finely grated
- ½ teaspoon kosher salt plus more for sprinkling
- 2 cups fresh corn kernels
- ½ jalapeño, seeded and finely chopped
- 1 scallion, sliced thinly
- Lime wedges, for serving

Preparation time: 15 minutes
Cooking time: 8 minutes

Directions:

1. Prepare fryer and set the temperature to 356 degrees. Cover the fryer with the lid.
2. In a food processor, add flour, eggs, parmesan, and ½ teaspoon kosher salt and pulse until well combined.
3. Add corn, jalapeño, and scallion and pulse 2-3 times.
4. When the temperature indicator light has turned off, add heaping tablespoons of mixture and fry for about 4 minutes per side or until golden brown.
5. With a slotted spoon, transfer fritters onto a paper towel-lined plate to drain.
6. Sprinkle with salt and serve immediately with lime wedges.

FALAFELS

Falafels are a Middle Eastern specialty made of coarsely ground chick peas shaped into balls and fried to a rich golden brown. They are packed with protein and make a handy snack on the go. Traditionally they are served with hummus or inside of a pita loaded with vegetables.

Ingredients:

- 1¾ cups dried chickpeas, soaked for 24 hours and drained
- ½ onion, quartered
- 2 garlic cloves, crushed slightly
- ½ cup fresh parsley leaves, chopped
- 1 tablespoon fresh lemon juice
- 1 tablespoon ground cumin
- 1 teaspoon ground coriander
- Cayenne pepper, to taste
- 1 teaspoon salt
- ½ teaspoon freshly ground black pepper
- ½ teaspoon baking soda

Preparation time: 15 minutes
Cooking time: 5 minutes

Directions:

1. Prepare fryer and set the temperature to 356 degrees. Cover the fryer with the lid.
2. In a food processor, add all ingredients and pulse until minced but not puréed.
3. With heaping tablespoons of mixture, make small patties.
4. When the temperature indicator light has turned off, fry patties for about 5 minutes or until golden brown.
5. With a slotted spoon, transfer patties onto a paper towel-lined plate to drain.
6. Serve immediately.

CRISPY GREEN BEANS

There is something about eating fried green beans that just seems healthier than eating French fries or onion rings. Go ahead and indulge.

Ingredients:

- 1 large egg
- 1 tablespoon baking powder
- 1½ cups water
- 2 teaspoons white vinegar
- 2 teaspoons garlic powder, divided
- 2 teaspoons salt, divided
- 3 cups all-purpose flour
- ½ teaspoon cayenne pepper
- ½ teaspoon black pepper
- 1 pound fresh green beans, trimmed
- Ranch dressing, for serving

Preparation time: 15 minutes
Cooking time: 4 minutes

Directions:

1. Prepare fryer and set the temperature to 356 degrees. Cover the fryer with the lid.
2. In a small bowl, add egg and baking powder and beat well.
3. In a shallow bowl, add water, vinegar, 1 teaspoon of garlic powder, and 1 teaspoon of salt and mix well.
4. Add egg mixture and mix until well combined.
5. In another shallow bowl, mix together flour, cayenne pepper, black pepper, remaining 1 teaspoon of garlic powder and 1 teaspoon of salt.
6. Dip green beans in egg mixture and then coat with flour mixture.
7. Repeat this process of dipping and coating once more.
8. When the temperature indicator light has turned off, fry green beans for about 3-4 minutes or until golden brown.
9. With a slotted spoon, transfer green beans onto a paper towel-lined plate to drain.
10. Serve immediately alongside ranch dressing.

Desserts

OREOS

Amazing is the only word to describe this mind blowing taste. Imagine warm, gooey Oreo filling surrounded by a hot, crispy, sweet shell. They really do melt in your mouth. Top with a sprinkle of powdered sugar and prepare for them to disappear fast.

Ingredients:

- 1 cup pancake mix
- 1 large egg
- 2/3 cup whole milk
- 2 teaspoons vegetable oil
- 18 Oreo cookies, frozen for 1 hour
- Confectioner's sugar, for dusting

Preparation time: *10 minutes*
Cooking time: *2 minutes*

Directions:

1. Prepare fryer and set the temperature to 374 degrees. Cover the fryer with the lid.
2. In a large bowl, add pancake mix, egg, milk, and oil and beat until smooth.
3. Dip Oreo cookies in egg mixture and coat completely.
4. When the temperature indicator light has turned off, fry Oreo cookies for about 2 minutes or until golden brown.
5. With a slotted spoon, transfer Oreo cookies onto a paper towel-lined plate to drain.
6. Serve warm with the dusting of confectioner's sugar.

CHERRY CHEESECAKE CHIMICHANGAS

This is just fun to say. You'll love eating them too, of course. They make for a beautiful presentation to serve to guests or just as a treat to yourself. This recipe makes 6 chimichangas. Serve with vanilla ice cream for a special dessert.

Ingredients:

- ½ cup plus 1 tablespoon sugar, divided
- 8 ounces cream cheese, softened
- 1 teaspoon vanilla extract
- 6 (8-inch) soft flour tortillas
- 1½ cups cherries from cherry pie filling
- 1 tablespoon ground cinnamon

Preparation time: 15 minutes
Cooking time: 3 minutes

Directions:

1. Prepare fryer and set the temperature to 338 degrees. Cover the fryer with the lid.
2. In a bowl, add 1 tablespoon of sugar, cream cheese, and vanilla extract and beat until smooth.
3. Spread tortillas out on a smooth surface
4. Place cream cheese mixture in the lower third of each tortilla.
5. Place cherries in the center of cream cheese mixture.
6. Fold sides of each tortilla toward center and then roll up like a burrito.
7. With a toothpick, secure the roll.
8. In a shallow bowl, mix together remaining ½ cup of sugar and cinnamon.
9. When the temperature indicator light has turned off, fry chimichangas for about 2-3 minutes or until golden brown.
10. With a slotted spoon, transfer chimichangas onto a paper towel-lined plate to drain.
11. Coat chimichangas with sugar mixture and serve.

PEACHES

Sweet juicy peaches are one of the best fruits around, especially to fry and serve with ice cream. This is really a simple recipe to make. The most time consuming part is slicing and peeling. The peaches will cook fast, so keep a close eye on them. Serve with vanilla ice cream or whipped cream.

Ingredients:

- 1¼ cups all-purpose flour plus more for sprinkling
- 2 tablespoons sugar
- ¾ teaspoon baking powder
- ¼ teaspoon salt
- 1 egg
- ¾ cup milk
- ½ teaspoon vanilla extract
- 3-4 fresh ripe peaches, peeled, pitted and sliced
- Cinnamon sugar, as required

Preparation time: 15 minutes
Cooking time: 2 minutes

Directions:

1. Prepare fryer and set the temperature to 374 degrees. Cover the fryer with the lid.
2. In a large bowl, mix together flour, sugar, baking powder, and salt.
3. Add egg, milk, and vanilla extract and beat until smooth.
4. Sprinkle peach slices with some more flour and then dip in batter evenly.
5. When the temperature indicator light has turned off, fry peach slices for about 1-2 minutes or until golden brown.
6. With a slotted spoon, transfer peach slices onto a paper towel-lined plate to drain.
7. In a bowl, place cinnamon sugar and peach slices and toss to coat.
8. Serve immediately.

BEIGNETS

Beignets are usually associated with New Orleans, but now you don't have to visit the French Quarter to try some. These pillowy mounds of goodness are great for dessert, breakfast, or enjoyed with a cup of coffee or tea. Be sure to use a heavy hand when dusting with confectioners' sugar.

Ingredients:

- ½ cup granulated sugar
- 1 envelope active dry yeast
- 1½ cups lukewarm water
- 1 cup evaporated milk
- 2 eggs, beaten slightly
- 1¼ teaspoons salt
- 7 cups bread flour
- ¼ cup shortening
- 3 cups confectioners' sugar

Directions:

1. In a large bowl, dissolve sugar and yeast in lukewarm water and set aside for about 10 minutes.
2. In another bowl, add evaporated milk, eggs, and salt and beat until well combined.
3. Add egg mixture to yeast mixture and mix well.
4. Add 3 cups of flour and mix until well combined.
5. Add shortening and remaining 4 cups of flour and mix until a dough is formed.
6. Place dough onto a lightly floured surface and with your hands, knead until smooth.
7. Place dough into a lightly oiled bowl.
8. With plastic wrap, cover the bowl and refrigerate overnight.
9. Prepare fryer and set the temperature to 356 degrees. Cover the fryer with the lid.
10. Place dough onto a lightly floured surface and roll into ¼-inch thickness.
11. With a pizza cutter or a knife, cut the rolled dough into 2-inch squares.
12. When the temperature indicator light has turned off, fry beignets for about 2-3 minutes or until golden brown.
13. With a slotted spoon, transfer beignets onto a paper towel-lined plate to drain.
14. Serve warm with a dusting of confectioners' sugar.

Preparation time: *15 minutes*
Cooking time: *3 minutes*

BANANA BITES

The secret to this recipe is using pancake mix. It makes for a nice, sweet batter that is really simple to make. The bananas become warm and gooey surrounded by a lightly sweetened fried outer shell.

Ingredients:

- 1 cup pancake mix
- 1 egg
- 1 cup milk
- 3 bananas, peeled and cut into ½-inch slices
- ¼ cup powdered sugar

Preparation time: 15 minutes
Cooking time: 2 minutes

Directions:

1. Prepare fryer and set the temperature to 356 degrees. Cover the fryer with the lid.
2. In a bowl, add pancake mix, egg, and milk and beat until well combined.
3. Dip banana slices in egg mixture evenly and let excess drip off.
4. When the temperature indicator light has turned off, fry banana slices for about 1-2 minutes or until golden brown.
5. With a slotted spoon, transfer banana slices onto a paper towel-lined plate to drain.
6. Dust with powdered sugar and serve.

APPLE RINGS

Hot, crispy apples in a matter of minutes. Use whatever your favorite apple may be. I like the Granny Smith because of the hint of tart that it provides, while my kids love the Honeycrisp for its easy sweetness. Slicing the apple into rings makes for a fun presentation, but you could also just use slices.

Ingredients:

- ½ cup flour
- ½ teaspoon sugar
- ½ teaspoon baking soda
- ¼ teaspoon salt
- ½ cup buttermilk
- 1 egg
- 1 large Granny Smith apple, peeled, cored, and sliced thinly into rounds
- Powdered sugar, as required

Preparation time: 15 minutes
Cooking time: 80 secs

Directions:

1. Prepare fryer and set the temperature to 338 degrees. Cover the fryer with the lid.
2. In a large bowl, mix together flour, sugar, baking soda, and salt.
3. Add buttermilk and egg and beat until smooth.
4. Dip apple slices in batter evenly and let excess drip off.
5. When the temperature indicator light has turned off, fry apple rings for about 20-40 seconds per side or until golden brown.
6. With a slotted spoon, transfer apple rings onto a paper towel-lined plate to drain.
7. Dust with powdered sugar and serve.

CARAMEL APPLE PIES

There is just something about the combination of apples and caramel that reminds me of fall. Perhaps it's eating caramel apples on so many past Halloweens. These mini pies use refrigerated biscuits, so they couldn't be easier to whip together.

Ingredients:

- 2 tablespoons unsalted butter
- ½ cup Philadelphia cream cheese spread
- ¼ cup brown sugar
- 1 teaspoon fresh lemon juice
- ½ teaspoon ground cinnamon
- 4 Granny Smith apples, peeled, cored, and chopped
- 1 package refrigerated biscuits
- 2 tablespoons powdered sugar
- ¼ cup caramel ice cream topping

Directions:

1. In a large sauté pan, melt butter over medium-low heat.
2. Add cream cheese spread, brown sugar, lemon juice, and cinnamon and cook until sugar is dissolved, beating continuously.
3. Fold in apples and cook, covered, for about 15 minutes.
4. Remove from heat and set aside to cool completely.
5. Prepare fryer and set the temperature to 356 degrees. Cover the fryer with the lid.
6. Place biscuits onto a lightly floured surface and roll each into a 6-7-inch circle.
7. Place 2-3 tablespoons of apple filling on each biscuit circle.
8. With wet fingers, moisten the edges of each circle and fold the circle over the filling to make a half-moon shape. With a fork, crimp the edges.
9. When the temperature indicator light has turned off, fry pies for about 2-3 minutes per side or until golden brown.
10. With a slotted spoon, transfer noodle squares onto a paper towel-lined plate to drain.
11. Sprinkle with powdered sugar and serve with the drizzling of caramel topping.

Preparation time: 20 minutes
Cooking time: 25 minutes

PECAN PIES

These miniature fried pies are sure to be the star of your next gathering. The crispy golden pockets are filled with warm, rich pecan filling. Serve on their own or with vanilla ice cream. Makes 24 mini pies.

Ingredients:

- 2 large eggs
- 1 cup light brown sugar, firmly packed
- ½ cup light corn syrup
- 5 tablespoons butter
- ¼ teaspoon salt
- 2 cups pecans, chopped
- 1 teaspoon vanilla extract
- 2 (14.1-ounce) packages refrigerated pie crusts, at room temperature
- Powdered sugar, as required

Preparation time: 15 minutes
Cooking time: 4 minutes

Directions:

1. In a medium pot, mix together eggs, sugar, corn syrup, butter, and salt over medium heat and bring to a boil.
2. Reduce heat to low and stir in pecans.
3. Simmer for about 8 minutes, stirring occasionally.
4. Remove from heat and stir in vanilla extract.
5. Set aside to cool.
6. Prepare fryer and set the temperature to 356 degrees. Cover the fryer with the lid.
7. Unroll both pie crusts onto a lightly floured surface and with a 4-inch round cutter, cut 24 circles.
8. Place a heaping tablespoon of pecan filling in the center of each pie crust circle.
9. With wet fingers, moisten the edges of each circle.
10. Fold the circle over filling and with a fork, crimp the edges.
11. When the temperature indicator light has turned off, fry pecan pies for about 1-2 minutes per side or until golden brown.
12. With a slotted spoon, transfer pecan pies onto a paper towel-lined plate to drain.
13. Dust with powdered sugar and serve warm.

MINI PEACH PIES

When peaches are abundant, be sure to make these little peach filled pockets for your loved ones. You will want to taste the peaches after they have been cooked in the skillet and adjust seasonings if needed. Some peaches may need extra sugar depending on their ripeness. Delicious served with a dollop of whipped cream or vanilla ice cream.

Ingredients:

- ¼ cup unsalted butter
- 2 cups fresh peaches, pitted and chopped
- 1/3 cup white granulated sugar
- 1 tablespoon brown sugar
- ½ teaspoon ground cinnamon
- ¼ teaspoon ground nutmeg
- 2 (14.1-ounce) packages refrigerated flaky pie crusts, at room temperature

Preparation time: 15 minutes
Cooking time: 3½ minutes

Directions:

1. In a skillet, melt butter over medium heat and cook peaches and granulated sugar for about 12-14 minutes, stirring frequently.
2. Remove from heat and stir in brown sugar, cinnamon, and nutmeg until well combined.
3. Set aside to cool completely.
4. Prepare fryer and set the temperature to 356 degrees. Cover the fryer with the lid.
5. Unroll both pie crusts onto a lightly floured surface and with a pint-sized jelly jar lid, cut into 4 inch circles.
6. Place about 1 tablespoon of peach filling in the center of each circle.
7. With wet fingers, moisten the edges of each circle.
8. Fold the circle over filling and with a fork, crimp the edges.
9. When the temperature indicator light has turned off, fry peach pies for about 2-3 minutes per side or until golden brown.
10. With a slotted spoon, transfer peach pies onto a paper towel-lined plate to drain.
11. Serve hot.

PEANUT BUTTER CUPS

From my father, I inherited a love for all things chocolate and peanut butter. This taste combination just can't be beat, and frying these candies that melt in your mouth is amazing. Freezing them for at least an hour will help the batter stick to them better. Be sure to make plenty for everyone as these will be a hit.

Ingredients:

- 1¼ cups flour
- 2 teaspoons baking powder
- ¼ teaspoon salt
- 1 egg
- ¾ cup milk
- 12 peanut butter cups, frozen for 1 hour
- Powdered sugar, as required

Preparation time: 15 minutes
Cooking time: 3 minutes

Directions:

1. Prepare fryer and set the temperature to 356 degrees. Cover the fryer with the lid.
2. In a bowl, mix together flour, baking powder, and salt.
3. Add egg and milk and beat until well combined.
4. Dip peanut butter cups in batter evenly.
5. When the temperature indicator light has turned off, fry peanut butter cups for about 2-3 minutes or until golden brown.
6. With a slotted spoon, transfer peanut butter cups onto a paper towel-lined plate to drain.
7. Dust with powdered sugar and serve warm.

FUNNEL CAKE BITES

Funnel cakes are always a favorite at the county fair, but usually about halfway through everyone starts to get a little stomachache from all the delicious fried sweetness. By making these little funnel cake bites, everyone can have the taste sensation of the funnel cake, but not the sick feeling of eating too much…well, maybe.

Ingredients:

- 1 egg
- 2 cups milk
- 6 tablespoons butter, melted
- 2 teaspoons vanilla extract
- 2 tablespoons sugar
- 1 teaspoon baking soda
- Pinch of salt
- 2 cups flour
- Powdered sugar, as required

Preparation time: 15 minutes
Cooking time: 4 minutes

Directions:

1. Prepare fryer and set the temperature to 356 degrees. Cover the fryer with the lid.
2. In a bowl, add egg, milk, butter, and vanilla extract and beat until well combined.
3. Add sugar, baking soda, and salt and beat until well combined.
4. Slowly, fold in flour until a smooth mixture is formed.
5. Place mixture into a sealable bag and set aside for a few minutes.
6. With a scissor, cut a small hole in the bottom corner of bag.
7. When the temperature indicator light has turned off, slowly squeeze some batter into small rounds in the fryer and fry for about 1-2 minutes per side or until golden brown. You can make the funnel cakes as small or large as you like as long as dough is frying evenly.
8. With a slotted spoon, transfer cake bites onto a paper towel-lined plate to drain.
9. Dust with powdered sugar and serve warm.

CHURROS

I think the first time I had churros was when we took the kids to Disney World. They were served with a chocolate dipping sauce and man, were they good! Creating churros at home with your T-Fal is really simple. Serve with your favorite sauce for dipping, such as chocolate or caramel.

Ingredients:

- ½ cup unsalted butter
- 1 cup water
- 1 tablespoon sugar
- ¼ teaspoon salt
- 1 cup flour
- 3 large eggs
- Cinnamon sugar, for serving

Preparation time: 15 minutes
Cooking time: 8 minutes

Directions:

1. In a pan, add butter, water, sugar, and salt and bring to a boil.
2. Reduce the heat to low and stir in flour.
3. Cook till dough becomes a bit dry, stirring continuously.
4. Remove from heat and set aside to let dough cool for about 10-15 minutes.
5. Prepare fryer and set the temperature to 356 degrees. Cover the fryer with the lid.
6. After cooling, add eggs to the dough, one at a time, and mix well between each addition.
7. Transfer the dough into a large sealable bag fitted with a large star tip.
8. When the temperature indicator light has turned off, squeeze dough in 3-4 inch lengths from the pastry bag and fry for about 2 minutes or until golden brown.
9. With a slotted spoon, transfer churros onto a paper towel-lined plate to drain.
10. Coat each churro with cinnamon sugar and serve.

TWINKIES & STRAWBERRY TOPPING

The Twinkie is such a nostalgic treat. They've been in production since the 1930s for crying out loud. It seems only American to make them even more delicious by deep frying them. The strawberry topping is the perfect accompaniment. You can use fresh or frozen strawberries, but frozen strawberries will have more liquid and may make the Twinkie soggy.

Ingredients:

For Strawberry Topping:

- 2 cups fresh strawberries, hulled and halved lengthwise
- 1/3 cup sugar
- 1 teaspoon vanilla extract

For Twinkies:

- Twinkies, as required (frozen overnight)
- 1 cup milk
- 1 tablespoon olive oil
- 1 tablespoon vinegar
- 1 cup all-purpose flour
- 1 teaspoon baking powder
- ½ teaspoon salt
- Powdered sugar, for topping

Preparation time: *15 minutes*
Cooking time: *10 minutes*

Directions:

1. Prepare fryer and set the temperature to 356 degrees. Cover the fryer with the lid.
2. For topping: In a pan, add strawberries, sugar, and vanilla extract over medium heat and bring to a gentle simmer. Cook for about 5 minutes, stirring continuously. Remove from heat and set aside to cool.
3. In a bowl, add milk, oil, and vinegar and mix well.
4. In another bowl, mix together flour, baking powder, and salt.
5. Add milk mixture into flour mixture and mix until smooth.
6. Dip Twinkies into batter evenly.
7. When the temperature indicator light has turned off, fry Twinkies for about 3-4 minutes or until golden brown.
8. With a slotted spoon, transfer Twinkies onto a paper towel-lined plate to drain.
9. Top with strawberry sauce and powdered sugar and serve.

BITE SIZED CANDY BARS

Serving up fried mini candy bars is the perfect late night snack for your sweet tooth. Freeze them overnight before frying and keep a close eye on them as they will cook quickly.

Ingredients:

- 1 egg
- 1 cup milk
- Pinch of salt
- 1½ cups flour
- Mini candy bars, as required (frozen overnight)
- Powdered sugar, for dusting

Preparation time: 15 minutes
Cooking time: 3 minutes

Directions:

1. In a large bowl, add egg, milk, and a pinch of salt and beat until well combined.
2. Add flour and beat until smooth.
3. Refrigerate the mixture for at least 30 minutes.
4. Prepare fryer and set the temperature to 356 degrees. Cover the fryer with the lid.
5. Dip frozen candy bars into chilled batter and cover completely.
6. When the temperature indicator light has turned off, fry candy bars for about 2-3 minutes or until golden brown.
7. With a slotted spoon, transfer candy bars onto a paper towel-lined plate to drain.
8. Dust with powdered sugar and serve.

Made in the USA
Middletown, DE
07 April 2019